MINI

Other Titles in the Crowood AutoClassics Series

MINI

James Ruppert

First published in 1997 by
The Crowood Press Ltd
Ramsbury, Marlborough
Wiltshire SN8 2HR

British Library Cataloguing-in-Publication Data
A catalogue record for this book is available from the British
Library.

ISBN 1 86126 047 4

Dedication

This book is dedicated to the new Mini in my life: daughter
Olivia Katherine Ruppert.

Typeface used: New Century Schoolbook.

Edited and designed by
D & N Publishing
Membury Business Park, Lambourn Woodlands
Hungerford, Berkshire.

Printed and bound by The Bath Press

Contents

Mini Thanks

Peter Burton when he was at Crowood Press. Brian Luff who gave me many Mini pictures and explained Issigonis from the engineer's perspective. *Car Magazine* for allowing me to dip into their archive, in particular Nick Elsden and Richard Bremner. Kevin Jones and Denis Chick at Rover for their help and Rover group copyright photographs. Pam Wearing who very kindly took me around Longbridge and introduced me to everyone on the production line, particularly Geoff Powell and Brian Dipple.

Gillian Bardsley, Karam Ram and Phillip Zanella at the British Motor Industry Heritage Trust. Brian Harper at Mini Sport Limited. Imogen Green at Leo Burnett Limited. Hornet and Elf Register, especially Lisa Baines, Jeffrey Allen, Nicholas Leviton, Russel and Alison Day. Tim Nuttall at the Moke Club. Richard Horne at the 1275GT register. At the Mini Cooper Register, Robert Young. Chris Cheal of the Mini Owners Club. Mark at Bank Garage for looking after my Mini. All those who allowed me to photograph their Minis, including Clive Powell and his wonderful Crayford Cooper Convertible, Kate Perrins and her immaculate 1275GT and Lynn Thompson's unique Mini Minor. Also Malcolm Harbour who had a pristine Moke and much to say about his years as a senior manager at Rover. British Motor Industry Trust have asked me to point out that all archive photographs are their copyright.

Apologies to my Mini Cooper, which took seventeen years to sort out. Thanks to my sister Marion for selling me her old Surf Blue 850cc Mini in 1977 for £50. My mother and father for putting up with lots of Mini bits around their house over the years. Finally my wife Dee, who also tolerates a lot of Mini-related nonsense and helped to check the text.

Introduction

It is classless, yet classy. It is small, yet perfectly formed. It is cute, it is cheap to run and buy used, it is a British institution, it is a Mini. We have all learned to drive in, dented, overloaded, got a lift from and attempted to make love in a Mini. If not, why not? At some time or other a Mini will affect your motoring life, probably for ever.

As a blueprint for a small car, nothing else is more suited to the cut and thrust of heavy traffic, or the perils of precision parking in a built up area. It is even fun to drive with sports car like steering, light weight and a willing engine, hence the Cooper and hence its astonishing competition success. Clearly the Mini has never stopped being a cheeky and chic little car; which may have been launched in 1959 but has yet to reach its sell-by date. The incredible thing is not just the fact that the Mini has managed to survive this long, but that it is built in the same place, in the same way, in some cases by people who have spent their entire working lives on the Mini production line.

The story of the Mini is also the story of a remarkable man, Alec Issigonis. Never before has one engineer's theories been so comprehensively expressed in real steel as with the Mini. Not only was it a brilliant package, but an eccentric one too. The lack of a proper location for a radio and the involuntary fondle of your passenger's knees when it was located uncomfortably far away underneath the dashboard was due to that fact that Issigonis did not like radios. They were a distraction. In his files at the British Motor Industry Heritage Trust are dozens of notes by the great man lamenting the passing of sliding windows. Issigonis was right, wind-down windows robbed the interior of so much useful space, but the Mini had to change.

Obviously the Mini is not a sensible small car buy any more. Other larger, hatchback cars are more practical, faster, frugal and civilized, but none have starred in a feature film with Michael Caine or won the Monte Carlo Rally. Except in the Ferrari, Morgan and Aston Martin factories it would be hard to find workers with such a passion for the cars they build. No wonder replacing the Mini is proving difficult. Brian Dipple, who has been on the production line since 1960, said he would retire when the Mini did, 'and that won't happen.'

He could be right. A new model to arrive at or around the Millennium may be badged 'Mini', but for millions of owners and enthusiasts around the world there will always and only ever be just one Mini. Here is the complete story.

MORRIS · **Morris S COOPER** · **COOPER** · **AUSTIN COOPER** · **Austin**

COOPER (1961-64) 997cc
LONG STROKE ENGINE · TWIN CARBS ·
FRONT DISC BRAKES · HIGHER FINAL
DRIVE · CLOSE RATIO GEARBOX
REMOTE GEARCHANGE · WIDER
DUNLOPS · BUMPER CORNER BARS ·
DUOTONE PAINT · TWO TONE TRIM ·
100 MPH SPEEDOMTER

COOPER S (1963-64) 1071cc
SPEC. AS COOPER · BIGGER DISCS ·
VENTILATED 3·5/4·5" WHEELS · FRESH
AIR HEATER · 120 MPH SPEEDOMETER ·
TWO TONE FLECKED UPHOLSTERY

COOPER S (1964-65) 970cc
JUST 963 PRODUCED · HYDROLASTIC
FROM SEPT '64 · SPEC AS 1071cc

COOPER S (1964-67) 1275cc ·
130 MPH SPEEDOMETER · 1965 4·5"
RIMS · 1966 TWIN FUEL TANKS · OIL
COOLER · HIGHER RATE HYDROLASTIC

COOPER (1964-67) 998cc FROM
ELF/HORNET PRODUCING 55 BHP ·
SEPT 1964 HYDROLASTIC SUSPENSION

COOPER S MK II (1967-70) 1275cc ·
REVISED AS OTHER MINIS & COOPER ·
SYNCHROMESH GEARBOX FROM LATE '68

COOPER S MK III (1970-71) 1275cc
REVISED MK III BODYSHELL · DOOR
TRIM/SEATS FROM CLUBMAN ·
HYDROLASTIC RETAINED

COOPER MK II (1967-69) REVISED
MARK II SHELL · INTERIOR AS SUPER
DE LUXE · NO BUMPER CORNER BARS

COOPER (1996-) BRANDED AS
'MINI COOPER' · FRONT MOUNTED
RADIATOR · REVISED FRONT SUBFRAME ·
ELECTRIC FAN · MULTI POINT FUEL
INJECTION · HIGHER FINAL DRIVE
RATIO · DRIVER'S AIRBAG · SEAT BELT
PRE-TENSIONERS · DOOR BEAMS ·
NEW STEERING COLUMN AND STALKS ·
SPOT LAMPS · BONNET STRIPES ·
ALLOY WHEELS · RETRO SPEC OPTIONS
'SPORTS PACK' 13"x6J ALLOYS · WIDER
ARCHES · KONI SHOCK ABSORBERS ·
AUXILIARY LAMPS · CHROME TAILPIPE
FINISHER · OIL/TEMP/BATTERY GAUGES

COOPER (1990-96) PRODUCTION MODEL
MINUS BONNET STRIPES, SUNROOF
LEATHER OR DRIVING LAMPS · JOHN
COOPER S 78 BHP CONVERSION KIT ·
1991 1·3i WITH CATALYST.

COOPER LIMITED EDITION (1990)
1275cc MG METRO ENGINE · 61 BHP ·
ALLOYS · BRITISH RACING GREEN · RED ·
BLACK WITH WHITE ROOF · TINTED
GLASS · DRIVING LAMPS · CHROME
GRILLE · BONNET STRIPES + JOHN
COOPER SIGNATURE · COLOUR KEYED
MIRRORS · WHEELARCHES · BLACK
LEATHER TRIM · RED CARPETS · RED
LEATHER STEERING WHEEL.

Austin · WOLSELEY · Mini · Riley · MORRIS

COMMERCIALS · VAN (1960-83) ¼ TON VAN BASED ON MINI FLOOR PAN WITH 4" EXTRA WHEELBASE AND 9.5" LONGER · REAR SUSPENSION STIFFER & LONGER TURRETS · 1967 OPTIONAL 998cc · 1969 REBADGED MINI VAN, 1978 REBADGED MINI 95 **PICK UP** (1961-83) AS VAN 1980 850cc ENGINE DISCONTINUED

MINI MINOR · SEVEN (1959-67) 850cc · STANDARD & DE LUXE TRIM · 1964 HYDROLASTIC SUSPENSION · 1965 AUTOMATIC TRANSMISSION OPTION

RILEY ELF · WOLSELEY HORNET (1961-69) 850cc · 8.5" LONGER · 1963 MK II 998cc · BETTER BRAKES COUNTER BALANCED BOOT LID · 1964 HYDROLASTIC · 1966 MK III REVISED INTERIOR · WIND-UP WINDOWS · CONCEALED DOOR HINGES

MOKE (1964-68) MILITARY PROJECT CIVILIANISED WITH 80" WHEELBASE 850cc BADGED EITHER AUSTIN OR MORRIS · MOST EXPORTED ·

AUSTIN · MORRIS MK II (1967-69) MINI 850 · MINI 1000 (998cc) · LARGER REAR WINDOW · SQUARE REAR LIGHT CLUSTERS · OBLONG GRILLE · 1000 IN SUPER DE LUXE TRIM ·

MINI MK III (1969-92) BADGED AS 'MINI' · LARGER DOORS · CONCEALED HINGES · WIND-UP WINDOWS · RUBBER SUSPENSION · 850 DISCONTINUED SEPT 1980 · 1982 METRO 'A' PLUS UNIT · 1984 12" WHEELS & DISC BRAKES

TRAVELLER · COUNTRYMAN (1960-69) 850cc · 10" LONGER · WOODEN BATTENS · 1962 CHEAPER ALL METAL MODEL · 1967 MK II FRONT END REVISED AS SALOON · 998cc STANDARD

1.3 (1992-96) 1275cc · 3 WAY CATALYST · SPRITE & MAYFAIR · 1993 METRO SEATS · INTERNAL BONNET RELEASE · MAYFAIR GETS FULL WIDTH WALNUT FASCIA

MINI (1996-) BRANDED 'MINI' · 1275cc MPI ENGINE · DRY COIL IGNITION · FRONT MOUNTED RADIATOR · ELECTRIC FAN · HIGHER FINAL DRIVE RATIO · DRIVER'S AIRBAG · SEAT BELT PRE TENSIONERS · DOOR SIDE BEAMS · WOOD FASCIA · ROOF AERIAL · NEW STEERING COLUMN & STALKS · LEATHER GEARKNOB · PLUS LOTS OF RETRO SPECIFICATION OPTIONS ·

CLUBMAN (1969-80) 998cc SALOON/ESTATE + 1275 GT · HYDROLASTIC · 1971 RUBBER · 1975 1098cc · 998cc AUTOMATIC

CABRIOLET (1991-96) LIMITED EDITION (75) BASED ON COOPER BUILT BY LAMM IN GERMANY · ROVER/KARMANN ENGINEERED MODEL FROM '93 AND BASED ON COOPER 1.3i

© 1996 JAMES RAPPERT

1   Baby Boom – Origins and Development

'God damn these bloody awful bubble cars. We must drive them out of the streets by designing a proper miniature car.'

Leonard Lord to Issigonis, March 1957

Alec Issigonis and the Mini are inseparable and synonymous. You can't have one without the other – the genius and his masterpiece.

One man with one automotive vision is a rare thing these days. There are plenty of other bodies waiting to get in the way of an innovative car: opinionated stylists, mad marketing gurus, cautious corporate bean counters, confused customer clinics. No wonder the majority of vehicles are bland and boring. If it is impossible today to find a single person guiding the development of a new car, in the 1950s it was equally rare to find a mass market player like the British Motor Corporation (BMC) entrusting a design brief to just one man. But that is exactly what happened. Alexander Arnold Constantine Issigonis did not know it in 1956, but he was about to make history and invent the modern motor car.

ISSIGONIS – THE EARLY YEARS

Born in the Greek city of Smyrna in 1906, Issigonis had a cosmopolitan background, his father being a naturalized Briton of Greek descent while his mother was German. The family maintains a close connection with the motor industry through BMW Chairman Bernd Pischetsrieder, ultimately controller of Rover's destiny.

In 1922 Issigonis came to England with his widowed mother, having lost their home as a result of war between Turkey and Greece – Smyrna (Izmir) is now part of Turkey. Setting up home in London, Issigonis enrolled at Battersea Polytechnic to study automotive engineering. After graduating in 1928 he joined a London design office run by Edward Gillet and worked as draughtsman and salesman on a project to incorporate an automatic clutch release on the gear stick. However, the Rootes Group proved to be more interested in Issigonis and in 1933 he went to Coventry to work for them, concentrating on independent suspension systems for Humber and Hillman. Issigonis furthered his suspension credentials at Morris Motors in Cowley from 1936. He was responsible for an independent front suspension system that was tested on a Morris Ten in 1939, but because of the outbreak of war was not seen in production until 1947 on the MG Y-Type.

During hostilities he worked on a number of projects for the war department. A priority, though, was a new small Morris car. Work began in 1942 on what was initially

Sir Alec Issigonis, genius designer and inveterate sketcher of brilliant ideas. No scrap of paper was safe from his cartoons, in the Leonardo da Vinci sense of the word.

known as the 6hp and soon after code named 'Mosquito'. This radical design incorporated a large number of important innovations. The body construction was unitary rather than the conventional separate chassis. At the front was independent suspension with torsion bars, plus responsive rack and pinion steering. Its engine was placed ahead of the front axle and the car ran on smaller than normal 14in wheels. The styling was heavily influenced by the 1941 Packard Clipper, the most up-to-date motor car of the period. Although the power plant was scheduled to be a flat four engine, the existing Morris 8 unit was installed to keep costs down. For aesthetic and practical reasons, Issigonis carved up the prototype and

inserted an extra 4in (102mm) width into the prototype. This last-minute action dramatically improved the interior accommodation and exterior proportions.

The first Issigonis masterpiece had been born. The Morris Minor was one of the stars of the 1948 London Motor Show and went on to become Britain's most popular car. During its long life of 23 years, the basic concept changed very little. Power plants were updated a couple of times, but essentially Issigonis had the concept right first time, a trick he was to repeat with the Mini. With the Morris Minor he touched an important nerve with buyers who wanted simple transportation, but also appreciated the lively handling, reliability and durability.

Despite this success, Issigonis left Morris in 1952 for Alvis in Coventry. There he worked on a large saloon that was the antithesis of the Minor. This V8-engined car had many innovative features including hydraulic interconnected rubber suspension units that were developed by Alex Moulton, a long time friend of Issigonis. However, Alvis shelved this saloon to concentrate on the more profitable production of army vehicles. Consequently Issigonis decided to leave in 1955 and took up an offer from Leonard Lord, the boss of BMC.

BABY CARS IN BLIGHTY

When Issigonis started to sketch the Mini he was following in the great British tradition of building small cars. Narrow roads, short journeys and a motoring public keen on economy are all conducive to small car culture, but the vehicle has to be a good one before it is accepted. Britain's own Model T, which revolutionized the previously expensive pastime of car ownership, was the diminutive Austin Seven. This is what Sir Herbert Austin had to say in 1929: 'I look back on the year 1922 as one that marks an important milestone in my life, for it was then that I introduced the now famous Seven, which has made motoring possible for thousands who could not otherwise have enjoyed its advantages. The Seven has done more than anything previously accomplished to bring about the realization of my ambition to motorize the masses. Of course, my little car was treated with a good deal of ridicule at first, but it cheers me up to notice that the appreciation that the Baby meets

Mini and its ancestor, the Austin Seven together. On this occasion John Coleman had just driven his 1925 Seven from Buenos Aries to New York, a journey of 11,647 miles (18,740km) and completed between November 1959 and July 1960. I am sure the Se7en would have been a little more comfortable.

today is just as hearty as the erstwhile smiles were broad.'

Austin could have been talking about the Mini. In fact there are a remarkable number of parallels between the development and success of the Seven and Mini. The two men were both practical engineers. Like Issigonis, Austin was responsible for much the of the car's design and both produced detailed sketches to express their ideas. Not only that, the prevailing economic circumstances in the post war 1920s and 1950s had similarities. Denied new cars, the public were eager to buy almost any form of transport. In the 1920s that meant a strange and unsatisfactory breed of vehicles called cycle cars, which were built by dozens of small firms. In the 1950s the emphasis was on economy after the Suez crisis and the country was flooded by mainly German two-stroke three wheelers, generically referred to as 'bubble cars'. What the Seven and Mini did was wipe out these small car pretenders at a stroke and motorize a group of the population that could not otherwise afford four-wheeled, four-seat transportation. In the words of Sir Herbert, 'A decent car for the man who, at present, can only afford a motor cycle and sidecar, and yet has the ambition to become a motorist. It is also for the vast hordes of motorists who realize that, owing to taxation and the high cost of living, they are paying ridiculously for the privilege of using their car.'

Like the Mini, the Seven became a British institution and went on to enjoy a glorious competition career. In fact, Issigonis built his Lightweight Special based on parts from an Austin Seven Ulster, which had independent suspension and rubber springing. The Seven even kick-started fledgling motor manufacturers, most famously and ironically BMW who built a version badged as the Dixi. It was even copied by Datsun, originally called Datson, prompting Austin to

The Duncan Dragonfly – the Mini's Grandad? Quite possibly. Transverse engine, front wheel drive and rubber suspension.

import a car to see if he could sue. Countless specials were based on the Seven, and the beautiful Swallow coachwork built by a little company called SS eventually turned into the mighty Jaguar concern. Certainly the automotive industry worldwide has a lot to be grateful for.

This brilliant little car was discontinued in 1939. Then the war got in the way of any model development, but there was an interesting interlude in the late 1940s when Austin bought a prototype car called the Duncan Dragonfly. This was a technically interesting two seater car powered by a transversely mounted two-cylinder engine that drove the front wheels. The suspension was rubber.

Instead of pursuing this ground-breaking concept Austin came up with the A30. As this prototype existed at Longbridge at the time of the Austin–Morris merger there is a strong suggestion that this vehicle could have influenced Issigonis when it came to devising a brand new small car. Surviving records curiously make no mention of this prototype and the part it played, if any, in the development of the Mini. Surely it is too much of a coincidence for an existing transversely mounted two-cylinder engined, front-wheel-drive car not to have had a bearing on a transversely mounted two-cylinder engined, front-wheel-drive Mini prototype that first emerged in 1957?

POST-WAR, PRE-MINI

Remarkably, Austin entered the post-war car market without a small car, which was almost unthinkable at the time. Their big rival Morris had already scored a huge success with the Issigonis-designed Minor. Then in the same year as the two companies merged, the A30 was unveiled at the 1951 Earls Court Motor Show. Like the Minor, it was virtually an all-new car and the body was the first unitary construction body built by Austin. Under the bonnet was a new overhead valve four-cylinder engine, which became known as the A series, and went on to power every small car from BMC to Leyland. Sadly, it was in a pathetic state of tune, as the 803cc unit developed just 28bhp. The A30 was less sophisticated than the Minor, although the independent coil spring and wishbone front suspension was a neat touch and much better than the Minor's complicated torsion bars and threaded trunnions. What let the A30 down most was the indirect worm and peg steering, which was less than a match for the Minor's rack and pinion. Interior space was at a premium with just 48in (1,219mm) of shoulder room across the front seats.

A range of A30 models soon emerged, with a four door saloon in 1952, followed by a two door a year later and in 1954 a van and Countryman Estate. Specifications were basic on early models: just the one windscreen wiper and sun visor, on the driver's side naturally, while the front windows were counterbalanced rather than having a complex winding mechanism and the rear windows were claustrophobically fixed. Not to miss a marketing trick, Austin called the A30 the new Seven. Obviously it was not. Neither was its successor, the revamped A35.

Austin at least dropped the pretence of calling the A35 a Seven. It addressed many

Austin A30. The first post war Seven, it was A series powered, but a little cramped inside. However, it proved to be useful on the track, especially in modified A35 guise.

of the original car's shortfalls, especially under the bonnet, when they increased the capacity of the engine by a massive 18 per cent to 948cc. Gearbox ratios were also revised and it became a much torquier and faster car. Whereas the A30 struggled to 60mph (97kph), the A35 romped up to 72mph (116kph). There were proper indicators rather than trafficators, the rear window was enlarged for improved rearward vision and all round it was a much better car. In all 546,672 were built and it proved to be a sturdily built and reliable little car. It was surprisingly successful in competition too. However, with the introduction of the Pininfarina styled A40, with its revolutionary two box shape, the A35 looked a little frumpy and twee. Its running gear having been successfully transplanted to the A40, the A35's days were numbered. Not surprisingly, it was discontinued in 1959 and replaced by you know what.

SUEZ + BUBBLES = MINI

Issigonis joined what was now BMC in 1955 and its Chairman, Leonard Lord, envisaged Issigonis devoting himself primarily to advanced product design. With this in mind a small team was assembled, including Chris Kingham and John Shepherd who had also been at Alvis. Jack Daniels, a brilliant draughtsman who had worked with Issigonis at Morris pre-war and had done the detail work on the Minor, was also an integral part of the team. The first project was a rear wheel drive family saloon that was to feature Moulton's Hydrolastic independent suspension with a two-box body. Code named XC9001, it was destined to be the 1800 model. A downsized version, XC9002, would eventually become the 1100. However, these projects were promptly dropped in March 1957 when a more important brief cropped up.

Sir Leonard Lord was offended by the sight of the mostly German produced bubble cars. The Suez crisis in November 1956 was the result of Egypt's President Nasser closing the Canal and Syria cutting the main oil pipeline that crossed their country. This crisis had ushered in petrol rationing and it looked like this dire situation would continue indefinitely. Not surprisingly, the British public put their faith in the economical, motorcycle-engined, three- and four-wheeled, plastic-bodied bubble cars. However, Lord reckoned that a small economical car did not have to be cramped and crude and told Issigonis so. His requirements were simple: BMC's small car had to be a full four seater, use an existing engine, be smaller than any company product (that meant the Austin A35 and Morris Minor) and should be introduced at the earliest possible opportunity. Issigonis constrained himself even further by mentally drawing a rectangular box measuring 120in (3,048mm) in length by 48in (1,219mm) wide and high. He decided that 80 per cent of this available space should be dedicated to the four occupants and their luggage, resulting in a passenger compartment of 102in (2,591mm). Out of that tight brief, which could have caused problems, came several brilliant solutions that made the Mini unique. The most obvious were the wheels, shrunk to an unusually small 10in (254mm) so that they did not intrude into the cabin. The suspension was also re-thought, as an independent system was always going to be a more compact package. There was just 18in (457mm) left to accommodate the power train. So a little lateral thinking led to the engine being mounted transversely, driving the front wheels via a gearbox and final drive built into the sump of the engine. Brilliant. All Issigonis had to do was make it work, in just two years.

Leonard Lord – The Mini's godfather

Born in 1896 in Coventry, the home of the British motor industry, Lord went on to become one of the most outstanding and successful car company bosses. His origins were humble, but he obtained a scholarship that got him to Bablake's, Coventry's old-established public school. The ambitious Lord worked initially as a draughtsman for Courtaulds and then went on to Daimler and Hotchkiss. When William Morris bought the latter company the exceptional Lord was difficult to miss and he was soon transferred from the drawing office to help reorganize Wolseley. From there he went to Morris.

Although Lord looked unassuming, with spectacles, a bald head and a cigarette permanently positioned in the corner of his mouth, he was a real corporate bruiser, 'If the door is not open, then you kick it open.' He fell out with Morris and switched allegiance to Austin. He transformed Austin's production methods and introduced important new models like the Big Eight and Ten. By 1950 he was in a position to propose a merger with his old firm. This eventually happened in 1952 with the creation of the British Motor Corporation.

Without Lord there would certainly have been no Mini. As the catalyst for the whole concept, offended by the sight of bubble cars, he asked Issigonis to come up with a solution that was exactly what Issigonis wanted: the smallest car with the largest payload space. Issigonis had only to produce some of his famously detailed sketches to get the go-ahead. Lord set an incredibly tight deadline, two years, yet got the production Mini in two years and one month. In part, this was due to the brilliance of Issigonis and his team, but the other crucial element was Lord's complete commitment to the project. He provided authority for anything that the team needed, which amounted to immediate attention from any part of the BMC organization. As he said to Issigonis after their decisive ride around the factory in the first prototype, 'I shall sign the cheques, you get on with getting the thing to work.'

Lord retired in 1961 to become Vice President and a year later was elevated to the House of Lords. 'Lord Lord would sound bloody stupid' was his typically blunt comment at the time, so he became Lord Lambury. His successor George Harriman respected his old boss so much that he left Lord's office untouched and unoccupied until his death in 1967.

ALTERNATIVE BUBBLE BUSTERS

Issigonis was not the only designer given a clean sheet to come up with a brand new small car. Leonard Lord did not get where he was without being very shrewd. Consequently he invited David Hodkin at ERA, the famous racing car company, which also did contract work for the industry, to work to a similar brief. He was aided by Laurence Pomeroy, technical editor of *Motor* and constant agitator for engineering change.

With Pomeroy acting as the ideas man, this pairing came up with the Maximin. This was a rear-engined, air cooled proposal with the engine cast in aluminium and mounted transversely. Interestingly, NSU arrived at the same conclusion with the 1000 just a few years later. For BMC though, the concoction would have been too costly and complex to build. The suspension was based on Firestone air bags with a constant height regulator, while an otherwise conventional gearbox was shifted automatically at set speeds. At least BMC must have thought that the name 'Maximin' had some potential.

Over at Cowley there was yet another project. BMC technical director Sidney Smith wanted to build a car for under £300. Charles Griffin responded with a rear-engined car powered by a two-cylinder A series unit. With high-silled bodywork and a sliding canopy in place of doors, they came in under budget.

Griffin was also in charge of yet another alternative Mini project a few years later, before the new car entered production. It was decided to think like the enemy and come up with a rival small car that would hit back at the Mini by being just as revolutionary and even better space utilization. He came up with the fascinating DO19, a one-box design that may have resembled the contemporary Fiat Multipla, but predicted the people carrier. The engine was rear mounted and the sliding doors were made of perspex. It was more roomy than a Mini, but considered dangerous in an accident with the front occupants seated far too close to any impact. Faced with all these alternatives, Lord picked the right one.

ADO 15 IS BORN

Initially the code name was XC9003, but this was eventually changed to ADO (Austin Drawing Office) 15. This was not the first time that Issigonis had experimented with front wheel drive, having studied contemporary Citröen and pre-war DKW systems while at Morris. For him, stability (especially with a small car) meant placing the maximum amount of weight over the driven

XC9003 – a very scaled down XC9001, but distinctively Mini and remarkably close to the finished article.

ADO 15, or more affectionately know to the testers as an 'orange box'. Here is one of the development hacks with an A35 disguise grille, which worked and also provided excellent access to the engine (which at this point was still the 'wrong' way round).

wheels. Issigonis even went so far as to build a front-wheel-drive Minor by turning the engine and gearbox through 90°.

The car was completed just before Issigonis left for Alvis in 1952 so there was not much opportunity to see how it performed. In his absence Jack Daniels had driven the car in ice and snow and found the handling remarkable. It worked because the driveshafts to the front wheels incorporated constant velocity joints. This design feature had initially proved to be a big problem as their original proposal had resulted in a hub bearing that was as big as a brake drum and consequently very heavy. However, MG designer Syd Enever sent Issigonis a drawing of a Hardy-Spicer Birfield joint. This turned out to be a part for submarine control gear, but proved to be perfect for adaptation into a vehicle driveshaft. Its origins could be traced back to 1926 and the Czech engineer Hans Rozeppa. Front wheel drive not only made sense as a concept, it was also a practical proposition for this new small car, but there was still a major problem to overcome.

Although there was enough room for an end-on gearbox in the Minor's big engine bay, the diminutive ADO 15 presented a big accommodation problem. The stroke of genius was to site the gearbox beneath the engine. A specially designed clutch went outboard on one side of the engine, and so

was still reasonably accessible. The differential gear for the final drive was built into the sump at the rear of the power unit. Equal length drive shafts incorporated inner universal joints and Rozeppa constant velocity joints at their outer ends.

A IS FOR A SERIES

There was no time to develop a brand new engine, so the power unit chosen was the well established A series, first seen in the diminutive Austin A30 in 1951. However, the team did experiment with a two-cylinder version by cutting the existing unit in half. In theory a smaller engine would save space and money, but in practice a two-cylinder A series performed very inefficiently and roughly. But with four cylinders, the 948cc engine proved to be dangerously quick for the time, and long before the Cooper had even been considered it was topping 90mph (145kph). As a result, the decision was made to cut the engine's output by 100cc.

Initially the carburettor and manifolding faced the front while the ignition and electrical equipment were positioned at the back. This layout was subsequently reversed for the production car. The official reason given was that this was warmer and stopped the engine icing up, even though later tests

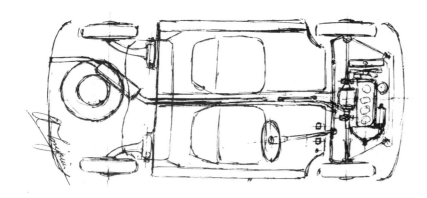

This early Issigonis sketch shows the familiar layout with a transverse engine, trailing rear suspension and radiator on the nearside, but no sub-frames.

revealed that there was only a very small temperature difference. However, the engineers discovered that the large primary gears between the clutch output and gear train caused too much inertia for the synchromesh to cope with. With the engine turned around, an idler gear reduced the size of the gearwheels.

Routine servicing could be tortuous enough in that tight bay on the production model, but hiding the electrics away would at least have stopped the little car drowning itself when negotiating puddles. Experiments with the gear lever placement included a dashboard mounting, which looked too quirky for British tastes, despite the 2CV precedent, and was also thought to be less than direct. However, once the engine was turned around and the lever located in its 'magic wand' position the change became even more vague. Only the later remote system restored the 'feel'.

DUNLOP'S DOUGHNUTS

An often overlooked yet crucial element in the overall success of the Mini were the tiny wheels and tyres. They helped keep the wheel arches down to minimum dimensions, increasing interior space. Small tyres reduced the car's unsprung weight and also helped it to look aesthetically correct. Issigonis could never understand why wheels needed to be so large, and during a meeting with Dunlop indicated with his hands just how small they should be. That gap was measured as 8in (203mm), but realistically the company settled on making tyres for a 10in (254mm) wheel. That was the easy part; making a small tyre that could cope with high rotational speeds, not disintegrate, provide reasonable tyre life, great grip and stay on the rim was going to be a challenge.

Dunlop proved to be up to the task. Revised compounds made the tyres durable. A tubeless design with a wide ledge meant better security and a safety shoulder dampened down the liveliness of the steering. Development mileage was racked up using a German Glas Goggomobil, because prototype Minis were unavailable at the time and the Glas had equally tiny wheels. Tyre development went hand in hand with the car's future success, from radial ply to rally winning Coopers.

Just as Dunlop had come up with well engineered and innovative solutions, Lockheed had to solve the problem of making the smallest hydraulic brake system to date. For the standards of the time, the performance was remarkable.

MORE DOUGHNUTS – RUBBER SUSPENSION

Independent suspension came late to the shores of Britain. Although it was popular on the Continent in pre-war years, the first British mass-produced car to have this feature was the Triumph Herald, launched in 1959. It was quite primitive, relying on transverse leaf springs and swing axles at the rear. By contrast, ADO 15 had rubber cones with fully trailing arms at the back. This was a joint project involving Alex Moulton, the Issigonis team at Longbridge and Dunlop who made the moulded rubber elements. Moulton's rubber cone system had been developed at Alvis and provided a clever solution to the problem of independent suspension, which could have intruded into the passenger compartment. The principle was that the doughnut-like circular rubber diaphragms were reduced to minimal thickness in the centre as they were compressed between two cones. One was attached to the sub-frame while the other was linked to a suspension arm. As a result this set-up produced a steeply progressive rate according to the number of passengers and weight of the luggage. In addition, rubber has excellent self-damping qualities, which decreased reliance on the dampers, making the whole system both light and compact. Issigonis had long been convinced of the inherent properties of rubber as a suspension medium, his independently sprung and rubber suspended Lightweight Special proving his point. He appreciated that for its weight the energy content of rubber was excellent, compact and cost-effective. Even so, the proposed Issigonis-Moulton system for the Mini was to have been based on interconnected reservoirs, but there was no time to develop it. Eventually the Hydrolastic system would be launched on the 1100 in 1962 and the Mini in 1964.

There was even some experimentation with a rear beam axle, although it proved too intrusive and would have reduced that 80 per cent of interior room fairly significantly. Even so, the Mini's amazing handling capabilities were no happy accident. Charles Griffin, the chief development engineer, can be roundly credited with creating the overall set-up. He experimented for a long time with the relative geometries at the front and rear of the car. As a result the rear wheels had a marked toe-in, which reduced understeer. Added to this was the highly responsive rack and pinion steering, which had done so much to make the Minor handle with such aplomb, though it was still considered unusual at the time.

STYLING? WHAT STYLING?

With all the mechanical problems addressed, Issigonis could get on with planning the bodywork, which from bumper to bumper was to be a mere 120in (3,048mm). Of course, the Mini was not so much styled as evolved around the mechanical components. Form

truly followed function. This really was minimalism, an intended but accurate pun.

As Issigonis once said, 'Styling is designing for obsolescence.' He was proved right by the Clubman, a late 1960s update that added length and a square front end for marketing rather than mechanical reasons. It was no surprise that the Clubman dated rapidly while the original 1959 design soldiered on undiluted. As Issigonis commented years later, 'The Mini was never meant to be styled. It is a functional thing … A car should take its shape entirely from the engineering that goes into it … The thing that satisfied me most was that it looked like no other car.'

So this shape was the smallest, simplest and most practical way of accommodating four people. The rounded panels looked natural while the external welding seams were incorporated for ease of manufacturing. Although it is true that Lord bankrolled the project, there were still strict budgets. Issigonis did not have enough money for jigs, so had to make his own, hence the seams around the roof and down the pillars. These are jigging ribs that allowed the car to be spot welded together cost-effectively.

Two-box styling was becoming a BMC trademark and was first pioneered by Austin with the A40 Farina model in 1958. The Mini looked fine with its tiny wheels at each corner and not an ounce of wasted weight or metalwork, but it was decided to increase the width of the body almost at the last minute by a further 2in (51mm) to boost interior room and because it looked right. Interestingly, Issigonis had made a similar late decision with the Minor although the extra 4in (102mm) was much more obvious because of a crude plate spacing the front bumper! Any lingering doubts that Leonard Lord might have had about the shape were dispelled by celebrated stylist Pininfarina who uttered an immortal phrase, 'Don't change it.' They never have.

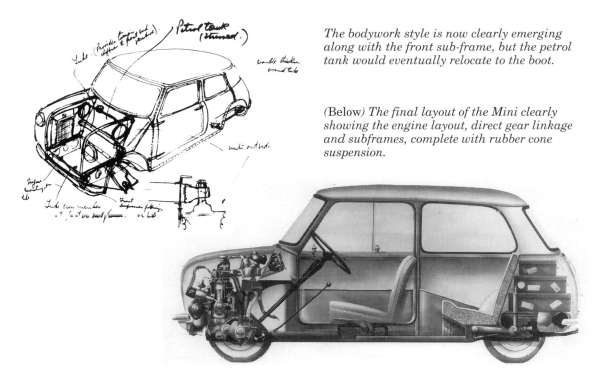

The bodywork style is now clearly emerging along with the front sub-frame, but the petrol tank would eventually relocate to the boot.

(Below) *The final layout of the Mini clearly showing the engine layout, direct gear linkage and subframes, complete with rubber cone suspension.*

TESTING, TESTING

The Mini took shape in a remarkably short time. Just four months from Lord's orders a wooden mock-up of the body and major mechanical parts were ready. By October 1957 two prototypes were already on the road. In July 1958 Lord took a test drive in the car and then told Issigonis to get it into production within twelve months. The first two prototypes were nicknamed 'orange boxes' because of their bright colour scheme and were sent to work at Chalgrove aerodrome.

Negotiating the poor perimeter road during a 30,000-mile (48,270km), 500-hour test led to a major revision of the design. Although the bodywork was going to be unitary, it was decided to fit sub-frames front and rear to accommodate the power unit and suspension. The original arrangement involved bolting and welding these parts to the bodywork, but dangerous metal fatigue set in. The sub-frame solution also helped to isolate the passenger compartment from the worst of the vibration and noise caused by the engine and road conditions. Also it was found that while braking on a downhill slope the rear wheels were unweighted and locked up. A brake limiter was introduced – only 40psi pedal pressure was needed to stop the car within 75ft (23m) at 30mph (48kph) – to improve weight distribution and balance. The battery, which had been located under the bonnet, was moved to the boot: yet another reason for the Mini's excellent handling.

Despite the tight time scale, pre-production testing was very thorough. Some problems did emerge though. There was a slipping clutch caused by oil from the sump getting onto the plates. Noise was still getting into the passenger compartment (via the gear lever this time). Torque steer made the steering somewhat lively under acceleration. And then there was that unusually hot and dry summer of 1959.

2 The Legend is Launched – Mark I

'Posterity will ... regard 26 August 1959 as a landmark in the development of the popular car.'

BMC press release

According to Mini legend the first example was hand built by production foreman Albert Green. The order had come through from George Harriman to build three proto-type cars. A new assembly line at Long-bridge was earmarked for production, but no workers had been allocated to it. There was no alternative; Green, along with his chief inspector Freddie Finch, set about the task. Green laid out all the components adjacent to 220 yards of assembly line and worked his way along it.

Evolution of the species? From the left, Kay Petre's Austin 7 racer next to Issigonis' Lightweight Special with its rubber suspension and just in shot, the Mini.

Seven hours later, the car was driven off the line by Green – chassis number 101, engine number 101, painted white, destined to be registered 621 AOK and become the most famous Mini of them all. But in the week ending 4 April it was one of just two pre-production prototypes to emerge and it still had an awful lot to prove. Nothing happened at the Cowley Plant in Oxford until ten Minis were built during the week ending 9 May. Now that production had started, preparations could be made for the launch of this remarkable little car.

Managing Director George Harriman had first teased the press at a 1957 Motor Show luncheon in London by stating that BMC's statisticians and market researchers had discovered that the public did not want bubble cars, but a low priced, fully engineered car. 'Obviously if the Corporation can produce such a car which will sell more cheaply, they will do so.'

BMC'S SECRET WEAPON

The venue was the Fighting Vehicle Research and Development Establishment at Chobham, Surrey and the date was 18 August 1959. BMC had invited the world's press to drive their new small car. After the old fashioned A35, journalists were asked to marvel at the brave new world of the Mini.

This Army testing ground was a secluded location that would not pre-empt the public launch and there were winding tracks, all the better to demonstrate the Mini's superb agility. There was the chance to thrash around the track at speed where Grand Prix winning journalist Paul Frere had set an impressive 122-second lap time on the foreign press launch two days later. Not only that, there was the chance to tackle a one-in-four gradient from a rolling start. Then it was on to the skid pan to discover vice-free oversteer.

MINI GOES PUBLIC

As far as the public was concerned the Mini hit the headlines on 26 August. In keeping with the badge engineering principles of the time there were two distinct advertising campaigns for the brands. Both the names used on these all-new cars referred to a previous or current greatest hit, hence 'Austin Se7en' (BMC's graphic device) intended to conjure up an image of Austin's pre-war bouncing baby car. The 'Morris Mini-Minor' was of course alluding to the post war success of the rather larger Issigonis-designed Minor. The new car was to have been christened the Austin Newmarket in keeping with the county theme adopted by BMC at the time.

In the glamorous world of advertising the Morris Mini Minor was promoted as 'Wizardry on wheels! Far more room in far less space.' Alternatively, 'From Austin – a new breed of small car!' For once all the advertising puffery was backed up by hard facts that emphasized all the Mini virtues that the buying public would eventually come to appreciate: 50mpg (5.6l/100km), 70mph (113kph) or over, front wheel drive, independent suspension and a highly space-efficient interior. There was even a neat little plan view of the car to explain the east–west layout of the engine. Morris lied about the 'big holiday size boot' but otherwise the Mini delivered what it promised.

MARK I – SPECIFICATION

At its launch the Austin Se7en and Morris Mini-Minor were available in two levels of trim: basic and De Luxe. There were also just three colours per model for the first three years: Speedwell Blue, Tartan Red and Farina Grey for the Austin and Clipper Blue, Cherry Red and Old English White for the Morris. Another distinction between the two

BMC were keen to show off the internal space available in their new car, although this 1959 promotional picture may have been a little optimistic.

(Below) A sectioned Mini on display at the 1960 Earls Court Motor Show. A brilliant way to demonstrate that there was bags of room inside.

marques were the grilles: Austin versions had eight horizontal wavy bars, which were chromed, and Morris models had seven vertical and eleven horizontal bars painted white. The basic car had fixed rear quarter windows, a fixed passenger seat, rubber floor mats, one sun visor, cloth upholstery, no screen washers and not much else. Well, what could you expect for just £497?

An extra £40 bought you the De Luxe version and not surprisingly the vast majority of Mini buyers opted for the trim and

850cc (May 1959 to October 1967)

Engine

Type	Four cylinder in line; cast iron block transversely mounted in front
Capacity	848cc
Bore and stroke	62.94mm × 68.26mm
Output	34bhp at 5,500rpm
Compression ratio	8.3:1; automatic 9:1
Maximum torque	44lb.ft at 2,900rpm; automatic 44lb.ft at 2,500rpm

Transmission

Type	Front-wheel drive
Gear ratios	4-speed 3.765/5.317/8.176/13.657 13.657 (reverse) (final drive)

Suspension

Front	Wishbones, rubber cones, Armstrong dampers; Hydrolastic from 1964
Rear	Trailing arms, rubber cones, Armstrong dampers; Hydrolastic from 1964
Steering	Rack and pinion

Brakes   Hydraulic drum/drum

Tyres/Wheels   5.2in × 10in cross-ply/3.5in × 10in

Dimensions

Track (front)	47.375in (1,203mm)
Track (rear)	45.875in (1,165mm)
Wheelbase	80.2in (2,037mm)
Length	120.25in (3,054mm)
Width	55in (1,397mm)
Height	53in (1,346mm)
Unladen weight	1,380lb (626kg)
Fuel capacity	5.5 gallons (25 litres)

Performance

Top speed	75mph (121kph); automatic 70mph (113kph)
Acceleration	0–60mph in 29.7 seconds
Fuel consumption	40mpg (7 litres per 100km); automatic 33mpg (8.5 litres per 100km)

Purchase price, 1959

Basic	£497
De Luxe	£537

Production

Austin	435,500
Morris	510,000

equipment of this model. Compared to the basic Mini, the interior of the De Luxe was almost sumptuous. It comprised two-tone vinyl upholstery, foam seat cushions, a vinyl covered dashboard, a chrome surround on the switch panel, fleck design trim, chrome kick plates on the doors, pile carpets, a rubber mat in the boot and head lining, which extended to the C pillars. The equipment level was just as dazzling – the front seat passenger benefited from an adjustable seat and sun visor. Fresh air was easier thanks to opening rear quarter lights, but there was less danger of freezing as a result of a heater and demister. On the outside, the De Luxe was just as distinctive. Chrome was lavished on the fuel filler cap, rear number plate surround and, on the Morris version, the grille. There were also bright plastic inserts in the windscreen rubbers and rear windows. The bumpers had overriders, the wheel trims were full width and the bright trim ran over both wheel arches and was joined at the sill.

MINIOMICS

At £497 the Mini was a cheap car, possibly too cheap. At the time the cheapest mass-produced car was the Ford Popular at £419 on the road. This was a dull, utterly conventional domestic appliance, with cart springs, a side valve engine and three-speed gearbox, yet the Mini was clearly being priced down to compete directly with it. The Mini also undercut its stable mates in the shape of the A35 by £41 and the Morris Minor by £93. More dramatically, it knocked the foreign competition into touch by being £116 cheaper than the Fiat 600 and undercutting the Renault Dauphine and Volkswagen Beetle by a whopping £219.

So the emphasis was on shifting units, which began leaving Longbridge at some 3,000 a week in an attempt to claw back some of the £10 million invested. John Barber, who went on to become managing director of British Leyland, was working as a senior accountant at Ford in 1959 and

1959 Mini in production. The body is lowered to meet the drivetrain and subframes. The same technique continues to be used in the 1990s.

claimed that the American company was so astounded by the low price they bought a Mini and took it to pieces. According to their costings it was impossible for BMC to make a profit, estimating a £30 loss on every one. Ford launched their completely conventional Anglia a year later, safe in the knowledge that at £93 more it would make money and appeal to a loyal core of committed buyers.

At the heart of the problem for the Mini was the fact the BMC still had not quite worked out exactly who was going to buy it. Issigonis had envisaged, quite wrongly, that this was a car for the workers. It was not; the complex mechanicals frightened them off. Potential buyers were scared of the technical advances and would rather stick with what they knew. Even a little further up the social ladder the aspirant lower middle classes were put off by the sight of an offensively small car. Small meant cheap, which it was. Not only that, there were plenty of well publicized teething troubles and for a while the Mini teetered on the edge of a very public and expensive failure. Strangely, it was saved by the press, high society and a bunch of racing drivers.

MINI REVIEWED

The reception given to the new small car was very enthusiastic. BMC's achievement in putting together such a revolutionary model at such an absurdly low price sent the press into raptures. This was not just a bunch of motoring hacks towing the patriotic line – they really meant it.

Motor Sport picked up on the new concept straightaway, identifying that they 'Seem to belong to a new class of family vehicle – dimensionally they are very small – in fact mini-cars.' The magazine went on to applaud the innovation of the design and the bravery of BMC in allowing a proper 'clean sheet' approach. After years of banging on about not being left behind by the continental competition, with some fresh thinking, the magazine

25 August 1959, the Morris Mini-Minor posed in a country setting.

Issigonis in the Mini. The extra internal space provided in the doors is clearly seen and was one of Issigonis's favourite features. Later Minis he drove were retro-fitted with sliding windows and door pockets.

(Right) *Loads of shelf space inside the new Mini-Minor.*

felt vindicated after being accused of having shares in Volkswagen's Wolfsburg factory. They were flabbergasted by the sensationally low price and summed up by conceding that

BMC 'appear to lead the world in small car design.'

Sporting Motorist joined the Mini fan club. They appreciated the fact that Issigonis was not about to sacrifice ride at the expense of roadholding. The magazine thought that the 'Accrued benefit from the rubber suspension and independent rear springing gives rear seat passengers the most comfortable ride we have yet experienced in a very small car.' Even in the wet they could corner the car on the limit with little roll and no hint that the car would break away. They found it quick too, 'With only one up the little car accelerates away in the most sparkling fashion.' They achieved better performance figures than BMC but admitted they probably had 'two up' at the time. Weirdly enough they were under the impression that the Mini had had an eight year development period. Obviously a BMC PR officer reckoned that no one would swallow the two years and one month truth! The magazine went so far as to inform its readers that they were planning to buy a Mini-Minor so that they could report back on the day-to-day pleasures to their readers.

Over at *Autosport*, John Bolster 'Knew at once that this would be by far the best machine that the Corporation has ever produced.' He liked all those features that for so long had been regarded as Continental, which meant independent suspension and front wheel drive. Not convinced by the styling, he believed that, 'One soon grows used to it, and the sheer good sense of its design appeals enormously.' The outstanding feature turned out to be the suspension, which despite the small wheels and poor road surfaces was 'superb'. The ability to corner at speed impressed, as did the quick, yet light steering. Overall he found the car well finished and despite the price, the build quality was not cheap. He concluded 'I am so happy that at last patriotism may be combined with enjoyable motoring, and I have expressed my appreciation by signing an order form.'

Autocar gave the car a dry write up, but still considered it to be outstanding. It set 'new standards of comfort and road worthiness in the very small family car class'. They saw most of its potential as a town car excelling in heavy traffic and proving to be easy to park. The magazine's editorial leader, however, was an enthusiastic endorsement of the new model in particular and front wheel drive in general. 'The road test report will gladden many hearts, for it offers great economy, lively performance, comfort for four grown ups and exceptional safety of handling, in a car costing home buyers around £500 total.'

Motor had an Austin Se7en De Luxe on test for 1,900 miles (3,060km) and reckoned that all the unconventional features: (10in wheels, rubber springs, transverse engine and front wheel drive) 'have justified themselves by results.' The biggest miracle was the packaging, in a car that could be so roomy.

In fact, a lot of journalists were interested enough to enquire what the delivery situation was like on this radical new car. Laurence Pomeroy – engineer, motor journalist, builder of a rival Mini prototype and author of the first and easily the best Mini book, *The Mini Story* – went a stage further and wrote to George Harriman suggesting that brother journalists should be given priority if they ordered a Mini. Harriman seized the opportunity and offered Minis on a twelve month loan with an option to purchase at a fair price once the period was up. The long term test car had been born. BMC certainly needed all the good press they could get. In all, eighty Minis were loaned out and they certainly got used.

John Bolster of *Autosport* reported back after six months of Mini-Minor motoring that although he was offered this extended loan he persuaded BMC to part with the blue car registered 981 GFC for cash. At the time of his report, Bolster had racked up a huge 10,000 miles (16,000km) in the UK and France. He suffered from damp carpet syndrome of course, but the service department apparently put that right. Otherwise it proved to be mechanically reliable, never missing a beat. 'Only an idiot or maniac could possibly have an accident.'

In short, the Mini-Minor proved to be nimble and practical. An interesting postscript to this piece was provided by Gregor Grant, who reassured readers that a Mini could cope with long distances. He took his wife and three children, aged 16, 14 and 9 to Scotland complete with luggage, much of it packed onto a Portarack roof rack. He clocked up 1,000 miles (1,600km), averaged 44mpg (6.4l/100km) and the Mini used no oil or water. He calculated that rail fares would have cost more than £22, whereas the petrol for the 810 miles (1,304km) from London to Glasgow and back was less than £4. Now if that did not convince readers of the benefits of Mini motoring, what on Earth would?

WATER, WATER EVERYWHERE

'It was a bit like having a damp Labrador in the back' commented an early Mini owner. The combination of water and carpets mixed to produce a soggy, musty and distinctly uncomfortable environment for anyone with their new Se7en or Mini-Minor. Longbridge could hardly believe the reports when they came through, as they had been very diligent in subjecting prototypes to water splash testing, but a brand new water splash was built outside the production plant to help solve the problem.

Several theories surfaced as the production process was scrutinized. There was the 'differential pressure theory' where it was suggested that a combination of an open window, the road and the interior created conditions conducive to the build up of moisture. Then it was pointed out that the prototypes had been hand-sprayed while the production Minis were baked, suggesting that the sealing material between the floor joints must have disintegrated.

The tendency of the Mini to provide its occupants with unwelcome foot baths was eventually traced to a late revision in the design. Originally, when the power plant was going to be smaller, a simple floor pressing with outward facing flanges was proposed. However, as the larger and more powerful four-cylinder engine was employed it was decided to strengthen the overall

---

Mini niggles

Never mind about periodic and unwelcome soggy sock syndrome, the original Mini owners also had a lot of other development work to do for BMC.

Ventilation The idea had been for air to flow through the sliding windows from a high pressure area around the windscreen pillar, and then depart through low pressure quarter lights. In fact the location was a high pressure one so they slammed shut. A locking window button soon stopped this. However, condensation was a worry until a fresh air heater in 1961 was added to the options list.

Window catches Chattering from the window channels was caused by ill fitting catches, which could even come adrift. They were re-designed.

Exhaust The downpipe fractured because it was used as a locating member for the engine on its mountings. The torque of the engine meant that it jumped about. So to stop the bottom bracket breaking, it was changed and the gauge of the downpipe increased while the rubber joints in the horizontal stabilizing bar were made stiffer.

Brakes The rear shoes in particular were prone to sticking in position and this was finally cured when Issigonis insisted on a heavy duty pull-off spring.

structure by boxing the outer edges. Unfortunately the floor pressing lapped the wrong way. The first quick fix involved taking a newly built Mini to an area of the assembly hall, where the sills were drilled and then injected with a heat-gelling foam sealer. It was cheap and not only stopped water going in, it also added a useful amount of torsional stiffness to the whole structure. The ultimate cure was a revised pressing so that the water entered the enclosed space and could then drain out again.

SUPER SMASHING

A very special Austin Se7en and Mini-Minor were launched in September 1961, clearly based on the contemporary Mini Cooper. The Super Se7en and Super Mini-Minor had a duo-tone colour scheme, with the roof painted a contrasting white or black. The Austin grille was a unique slatted version with twelve straight vertical bars and nine wavy horizontal ones and the Morris version had ten horizontal bars. However, the rest was pure Cooper: stainless steel window surrounds, sill finishers and bumpers complete with overriders and 'tubular extensions' (the corner piece sections). Inside, the trim was all two-tone, there were carpets, a boot board, extra soundproofing, a courtesy light and oval instrument binnacle. The Cooper touches extended to black faced instruments, chrome door levers instead of the string pulls and black vinyl on the dashboard. Mechanically the modifications were minor, the anachronistic separate floor starter was replaced by a combined ignition and starter key. The engine may have been standard Mini 848cc, but a Cooper 16-blade fan replaced the inadequate four blade item and was so successful in improving cooling and reducing engine noise that it was extended to the rest of the range within a few months. This is one of the rarest models. It remained in production for just over a year, to be replaced by the less Cooperish Super De Luxe.

In 1962 the 'Se7en' name was dropped for the Austin model – hardly surprising as the name conjured up a tiny, pre-war, vintage car rather than an iconoclastic model at the cutting edge of automotive technology. So it was dramatically re-badged 'Austin Mini'. The Morris Mini-Minor stayed the same; significantly, the 'Mini' part of its monicker had been plucked out as the defining name and would survive the already nebulous marque identities.

The Super De Luxe arrived in October 1962 and in spite of retaining overriders and tubular extensions on the bumpers it largely reverted to standard Mini specification with some chrome knobs on, to set it apart from the Cooper. Inside, there was the luxury of Vynide upholstery, chrome hinged sun visors and lidded ashtrays.

HYDROFANTASTIC?

The most significant change to the Mark I Mini occurred in September 1964 with the introduction of Hydrolastic suspension. First used on the 1100 range, it was the logical development of the original suspension. Rubber was still used as the springing medium, which linked the two ends of the car by transmitting the deflecting forces through fluid in a pipe. At the front, transverse links carried the front wheels, acting on Hydrolastic units housed in the sub-frame. When a road wheel struck a bump the tapered piston was forced into the cylinder and because fluid cannot be compressed, pressure was passed on to the conical rubber spring. The piston became larger as the diaphragm rolled off the walls of the cylinder on to its tapered crown, making the spring progressive so that it stiffened up at an increasing rate.

A sectioned Hydrolastic unit on show at Earls Court in 1964.

Damping was built in by forcing the fluid through a separating member between the upper and lower parts of the cylinder. The fluid could go through a bleed hole, which copes with small deflections, or through the two rubber flap valves, which operate as dampers for bump and rebound. The fluid used was 50/50 water and alcohol antifreeze with some rust inhibitor and even a Customs and Excise additive to make it undrinkable! Not only that, it would also not be affected by any changes in temperature. The same Hydrolastic units were at the back, but they were laid horizontally within the sub-frame and worked by bell cranks from the trailing arms. Pipes connecting the units run on each side of the car, rather than side to side, which meant there was a degree of resistance to roll. There were many minor improvements too.

The 1964 models received a number of further modifications. Inside, the interior light switched on automatically once the door was opened. There was an oil warning light and

October 1964 and the revolutionary Automotive Products automatic gearbox makes its debut at the 1964 Motor Show. The remote lever allowed selection of any of the four gears, or fully automatic operation.

for safety reasons crushable sun visors and plastic rimmed rear view mirror. Mechanically, the gearbox was strengthened to Cooper specification. The mainshaft had needle roller bearings instead of plain bronze bushes and wider teeth in the gears, while a diaphragm spring clutch and new speed change forks completed the transmission revisions. In addition there were twin leading shoe front brakes and, less important, the Super De Luxe was shortened to De Luxe.

DR ALEX MOULTON – SUSPENDED ANIMATION

The Mini was a team effort and a crucial member of that team was Alex Moulton. He met Issigonis for the first time in 1948 when they talked about Moulton's proposal to develop a rubber suspension system.

When Issigonis left Morris to join Alvis, the big car he designed for them, the Diablo, featured Moulton's rubber suspension. At the same time, Moulton was also doing work for Morris and with Jack Daniels, a prominent member of the original Mini team, he was converting a Morris Minor to use a new Flexitor rubber front suspension system. Meanwhile the Alvis was developed further when Moulton filled the hollow cones used in the suspension system and then linked the front and rear ones together so that the fluid could be displaced hydraulically. This was the beginning of the Hydrolastic and much later Hydragas suspension.

However, when it came to developing the Mini, there was no time to miniaturize these cones. The stop-gap measure was to cut them in half and use them as a sort of buffer. Moulton and Issigonis, though, still dreamt of using a much more sophisticated interconnected system. Hydrolastic suspension was introduced in 1964. Unfortunately, the system was expensive to produce and on

mainstream Minis was used only until 1969, although it was fitted to the Coopers until 1971 to use up existing units.

Moulton continued to come up with revolutionary suspension solutions that were sadly compromised by production or budgetary constraints. In 1973 the Hydragas system was fitted to the Allegro, which lacked sub-frames and prevented the inclusion of anti-dive and anti squat geometry. The system fitted to the Metro from 1990 regained its credibility. Moulton went as far as equipping his own 1966 Cooper S with Hydragas (spheres filled with nitrogen and connected front to rear) and A-shaped tubular lower suspension arms, rubber bushed and inclined to provide a degree of anti-dive. Rubber bushes on the upper transverse arm reduced road roar and also friction to the axially mounted bushes, cutting down road noise. At the back the rear suspension had a pair of slim helper springs just like Hydrolastic cars to prevent the rear end sagging under heavy loads. The result was a smooth and quiet ride.

Clearly there was and still is development room left in the original Mini and lessons to be learnt for the next generation of Minis. This probably explains why Moulton was co-opted to work with the team designing the all-new Mini for the Millennium.

MARK I LEAVES ITS MARK

An interesting new option from 1965 was four-speed automatic transmission, even though production did not start for some time. It proved to be very popular. *Autocar* tested one in October, when they noted the fuel consumption penalty of around 10 per cent and did not like the high price. Performance matched the manual car, with just a 2mph (3kph) sacrifice in top speed. There was nothing to compare it with except the unique and slightly bizarre DAF from Holland. By

As the millionth Mini rolls off the Longbridge production line, Alec Issigonis may feel proud, but he also looks a little pensive. After all, this million seller was not making a profit.

contrast with the Mini's four-speed torque converter based system, the DAF had driving belts on expanding and contracting pulleys with an infinite variation of ratios. That made the DAF system smoother, but hardly as versatile as the Mini. 'BMC's baby has developed into a much more civilized product than the original' they concluded.

The external door handles soon had small protective safety bosses to prevent pedestrians from being injured. These were first seen on Morris versions in 1965 and Austins in 1966. A new clutch meant a smoother operation while sealed beam headlamps became standard.

By 1967, when the last few Mark I models were leaving the production lines, the Mini had clearly come a very long way in eight years. It had started life as a technically interesting oddball. Sales were slow and the problems were plentiful, although a necessary evil of a short development run was a few post-production problems. However, BMC were quick to respond, fix the glitches and watch production climb rapidly from 19,749 in 1959 to 237,227 in 1967. On the showroom floor it was a big hit right from the start. As Bill Preston (now sales director at one of Rover's longest serving dealers, G. Kingsbury) remembers: 'So many people said to me, "you'll never sell that." They laughed out loud. Not for long though, we could not get enough of them, some people almost came to blows in the showroom when it came to allocating the first Minis.'

Other manufacturers were surprisingly slow to follow suit with their own 'mini' cars. Maybe they had good reason to be cautious, had done their sums and were biding their time, mindful of the aphorism 'mini cars make mini profits'. After all, Ford did not dip their toes in the small car water until 1976 and the supermini Fiesta.

AUTOMATICALLY MINI

At the heart of the quest for a simple, usable small car was an automatic gearbox. Issigonis had begun his career as the one and only draughtsman in a London based engineering consultancy trying to market a semi automatic gearbox, and this had obviously left an impression. The technology never existed at

the Mini's launch although Automotive Products were tackling the problem. A bevel gear device designed by Hugh Reid was the breakthrough as it acted like a torque converter to link the engine and gearbox.

A two-speed version, with no reverse, worked well in a Humber Hawk. Then the Austin A50 Cambridge was fitted with a three-speed system in which, like the Mini, lubrication was shared by the engine and gearbox. Just as the Mini was launched, Automotive Products saw the potential and created a three-speed gearbox only slightly larger than the manual version, which fitted in the same location. Issigonis was delighted, especially when an extra gear could be added at minimal cost. The clutch was replaced by a torque converter attached to the crankshaft. The drive was then transmitted by primary gears to the bevel gear within the transmission. Two clutches were

By the late 1960s there was a complete range with pick-up, van, Countryman and a range of saloons.

then employed, one for the forward gear, the second coming in when top was engaged, which also transmitted reverse. From the clutch, the power went to the differential, the driveshafts and then to the road wheels.

The disadvantages were minimal, though it cost £90 more. There was also a slight performance penalty despite a larger carburettor, caused by the power consumed by the torque converter, which depressed top speed and fuel consumption by around 10 per cent. However, this unit remained the only automatic gearbox in the world suitable for cars under 1.3 litres. Yet another Mini first.

Small cars before the Mini

The small car market that existed in the UK of the 1950s was a very strange one; lots of British companies in the 'never had it so good' climate had a crack at building small cars. What many of these models had in common were sundry motorcycle components, a plastic body, a complete absence of style and a silly name.

Most were not so much mini as micro cars. Take the Astra Utility (1956–60): originally badged as a Jarc, it looked like a little van and was powered by an under-floor Anzani engine and three-speed gearbox. Equally odd was its close relative, the Gill Getabout (1958). More successful was the Bond Minicar (1948–65), a three wheeler with a prescient name that originally had a front-mounted Villiers two-stroke motorcycle engine driving the single front wheel by a chain.

Then there was the Fairthorpe Atom (1954–57), a four wheeled British bubble car, and the BSA twin powered Atomota (1958–60). How about the Frisky Sport (1958–59), with its suicide doors, Villers engine and open top? Ugh! The Opperman (1956–59) had only its great economy going for it. The Powerdrive (1956–58) was a three wheeler with two wheels at the front, as opposed to the Austin Seven powered Reliant Regal (1951–62). The Scootacar (1957–65) was an upright egg of a tri-scooter at just 81in (2,057mm) long. The Tourette (1956–57) was another eggy design inspired by the German Mopetta, with a single chain-driven rear wheel.

British manufacturers were not the only ones cobbling together weird little cars; the Germans were also pretty good at it. The illustrious name of BMW was attached to the Isetta (1955–65), the quintessential bubble later built in the UK. The Glas Goggomobil (1955–67) was almost roomy, with Mini-sized wheels; BMW bought the company in the 1960s. The other offensive three-wheel bubble car was the Heinkel (1956–65), eventually built in the UK by Trojan. The Messerschmitt (1953–64) was a tandem-seat scooter, although the later Tiger had an extra wheel and a frightening amount of power. The Nobel Fuldamobil (1959–61), a classic egg-shaped three wheeler, was also built by Lea Francis in the UK. The French offered us the Vespa (1958–61), an Italian design that was built well in France.

The BMW Isetta. The Mini saw these bubble cars and other unstable tri-wheeled eyesores off the road by the early 1960s. Ironic, then, that BMW now own the Mini.

3 Makeover – Mark II

*'Carpets still do not lie snugly on the
floor – a criticism we made in 1959.'*

Autocar

Minutes before the press got to see the
revised Mini for the first time, something
vital was missing: the badges. They were
being sourced from Ireland: the cardboard
box containing them was sneaked past the
waiting journalists and frantic BMC staff
had to press them into place.

Slightly better organized was the 1967
Earls Court Motor Show, the public venue
for the launch of the Mini Mark II. The two
marques continued but with a further subtle name change as the Morris Mini-Minor
simply became the Morris Mini. There were
also prominent and no longer elusive
chrome Mark II badges at the rear to make
sure that everyone knew that this was the
brand new Mini.

For the first time in eight years the Mini
received a facelift. The visual differences
were obvious enough as the grille was
squared off with a much wider surround.
The grille itself featured eleven bars on the
Austin and thirteen on the Morris with
seven vertical ones. At the back the saloon's
rear window became larger and there were
new shoe box sized square light clusters. On
the road, drivers would notice the difference
when they tried to park. The turning circle
had been reduced from 32ft (10m) to 28ft
(9m) with modifications to the steering rack

and arms. Stopping became less strenuous
as increased bores in the brake cylinders
meant smoother, yet lighter action. Performance was improved too, because for the
first time the 998cc engine was made available in the standard Mini shell, having previously been fitted to the up-market Riley
Elf and Wolseley Hornet. This new 1000
model also benefited from the Cooper's
remote gear change and a higher 3.44:1
final drive ratio. The Automotive Products
automatic gearbox was improved and still
available as an option with the higher compression 9:1 engine.

Inside, a driver might have noticed safer
bezels on the instruments and a protective
foam filled roll on the dashboard. In addition, the switchgear had helpfully been
located 3in (76mm) further forward. Other
long overdue instrument changes included
the relocation of the floor mounted dip
switch to the indicator stalk, which also
housed a louder horn, while the flashing
indicator warning light was transferred to
the speedometer. And finally, those tiny
windscreen wipers were taught to park
themselves once switched off.

The 848cc model, now badged as the 850,
was still available in two levels of trim, basic
and Super De Luxe, while the 1000 came

The Mark II Mini, seen here in Super De Luxe trim, was distinguished by its reshaped grille with thicker surround – and that was about it, unless you specified a 1,000cc engine under the bonnet. From the rear it looked very different, due to the larger rear window, bigger light clusters and new badging.

only with the Super De Luxe trimmings. Like the Mark I these included opening rear quarter lights, overriders (but no corner bars), a three-instrument binnacle, ergonomically effective seats, a heater and carpets.

MARK II – REVIEWED

As far as the buying public were concerned the new Mini was more of the same successful formula. Sales were not going to be a problem. Motor journalists – always on the look out for a reinvention of the wheel – were a little disappointed, especially after the exciting innovations delivered by the first Mini in 1959. *Autocar* certainly regarded the availability of the proven 1,000cc engine across the range as important. They thought that the Cooper S final drive made a difference at high cruising speeds, while the remote control gear change, also from the Cooper, was a very welcome update. They liked the smaller turning circle and more effective handbrake.

Then came the regrets. Heating and ventilation were just as poor as the old model. Despite the fact that new seats were fitted, they lacked support to the thighs. Visibility may have improved, but the rear view mirror was still tiny. The view through the windscreen was not helped by the small

850/1,000cc (October 1967 to December 1969)

Engine

Type	Four cylinder in line; cast iron block transversely mounted in front
Capacity	848/998cc
Bore and stroke	62.94mm × 68.26mm/64.6mm × 76.2mm
Output	34bhp at 5,500rpm/38bhp at 5,250rpm; automatic 41bhp at 4,580rpm
Compression ratio	8.3:1; automatic 8.9:1
Maximum torque	45lb.ft at 3,450rpm; automatic 45lb.ft at 2,500rpm

Transmission

Type	Front-wheel drive
Gear ratios	4-speed 3.765/5.317/8.176/13.657 13.657 (reverse) (final drive) 4-speed automatic

Suspension

Front	Hydrolastic
Rear	Hydrolastic
Steering	Rack and pinion

Brakes   Hydraulic drum/drum

Tyres/Wheels   5.2in × 10in cross-ply/3.5in × 10in

Dimensions

Track (front)	47.375in (1,203mm)
Track (rear)	45.875in (1,165mm)
Wheelbase	80.2in (2,037mm)
Length	120.25in (3,054mm)
Width	55.5in (1,410mm)
Height	53in (1,346mm)
Unladen weight	1,400lb (635kg)
Fuel capacity	5.5 gallons (25 litres)

Performance

Top speed	72mph (116kph)/75mph (121kph)
Acceleration	0–60mph in 29.7/22 seconds
Fuel consumption	40mpg (7 litres per 100km)/34mpg (8.3 litres per 100km); automatic 33mpg (8.5 litres per 100km)

Purchase price

1000	£589

Production

Austin	154,000
Morris	206,000

windscreen wiper arc, which seemed biased towards the passenger. Overall *Autocar* were just a little disappointed, 'We were expecting the new Mini to be announced with winding windows, like certain versions built in Australia. This must now be the only car without them, and they are sadly missed. It is also time such economies as cable release interior door handles were brought up to date; and some of the standards of fit and finish were disappointing. Carpets still do not lie snugly on the floor – a criticism we made in 1959.' Nevertheless the magazine admitted that the Mini was still in a class of its own. 'When all is said and done, however, the Mini is a tremendously practical and dynamic little car that has few equals for town use, or as the second family transport.'

Always difficult to please, *Car Magazine* in September 1968 compared the new Mini 1000 with the increasing number of rivals. There was the obviously outclassed Reliant Rebel 700, the underachieving Hillman Imp and the exotic threat from the Far East in the shape of the Honda N600. It was the Honda that came closest to trouncing the British car as it was faster, more economical and cheaper than the Mini 1000. However they found it, 'Noisier and less comfortable with inferior handling. In so many ways it is so close to the Mini that as long as it holds its price at its present level it is bound to present a very considerable challenge.' They were not going to let the Mini off lightly after seeing the super mini future and the considerable Far Eastern threat. 'Of the Mini itself, one is bound to say that some of the room for improvement that we have always said existed is still there. Rather than the restyled grille and rear lights with which we were regaled last year, we would have liked to see a lot more attention paid to driver comfort by way of supplement to vast improvements in ride and silence.'

The short-lived Mark II was subjected to relatively few changes. In June 1968 the company replaced the convenient and ergonomically efficient door cables with fiddly door handles, possibly in response to *Autocar*'s road test comments. The only big news was that from September 1968 an all-synchromesh four-speed gearbox (first introduced on the Cooper S in 1967) was standard across the range.

Also in that year, as BMC merged with the Leyland truck makers, production of the Mini was halted at Cowley and transferred to Longbridge. The Leylandization of the Mini had begun.

MINIOMICS 2 – MAXI MERGERS

After the 'never had it so good' 1950s the new car market entered the highly competitive 1960s. This triggered a whole series of mergers, which overshadowed the industry during the decade. First, in 1960, Jaguar acquired Daimler. The following year Standard-Triumph was bought by Lancashire based commercial vehicle makers Leyland. Meanwhile, BMC had benefited hugely from the front-wheel-drive revolution led by the Mini and 1100, so output soared.

Unfortunately profits did not. BMC made a profit of £27 million on sales of £346 million, but by 1967 although sales had risen to £467 million, it recorded a loss of £3 million. Virtually non-existent product planning and chronic underpricing were to blame and forced the company to merge with Jaguar in 1966 as British Motor Holdings (BMH). Then Leyland – recent purchasers of Rover – came back into the picture. There was Labour government encouragement to merge with BMH. On 17 January 1968 the British Leyland Motor Corporation (BLMC) was born and became the world's fifth largest car company. Sir George Harriman was appointed Chairman and Sir Donald Stokes became Managing Director, while the ten board members were drawn equally from BMH and Leyland. Almost immediately there were problems as BMH was due to make a loss, but the merger went ahead anyway. Officially, BLMC came into being on 14 May 1968.

What Stokes found was an over-staffed, inefficient company. Profitability on the Mini was marginal and product planning was a haphazard affair with no clear model policy. The new management structure meant that the influence of Issigonis was on the wane. Appointed director of research and development, he was encouraged to innovate, though Stokes resented his dogmatic demeanour. Citing the Mini's sliding windows, Stokes claimed many years later that it was only pressure from the board that brought in the winding variety in 1969. Those Mark III changes were the last significant updates until the 1990s. The problem was that BLMC did not have any money to spend. The huge company had lots of other projects and lost causes and the Mini was the last priority. So the Mini remained stranded in 1969.

LIMP IMP

The Mini was not alone in the small car sector during the 1960s. The equally innovative Hillman Imp and its badge-engineered derivatives should have been a contender, but it failed dismally. Part of the problem was that it was launched after the Mini. However, the car's origins predated the Mini: Bernard Winter, Rootes' chief engineer, had allowed Tim Fry and Michael Parkes in the experimental department to dream up a small car. The 'Slug' was their basic answer, with a rear mounted two-cylinder air-cooled engine that was eventually replaced by an aluminium, overhead camshaft unit from Coventry Climax. Fry and Parkes both bought Minis and knew what they were up against. What Rootes eventually launched in May 1963 was a very sophisticated car that was quiet, economical and fun to drive. Not only that, the opening rear window and folding rear seats were innovative hatchback touches.

Unfortunately the Imp at £508 cost £61 more than the basic Mini. Not only that, building such an advanced car at a brand new factory in Scotland led to quality problems from an inexperienced workforce. The

The Hillman Imp, a Mini-come-lately that deserved to do well, but never matched it for reliability, performance or character.

Imp gained a reputation for unreliability because servicing garages were not used to dealing with the finer tolerances of an aluminium engine. Automatic chokes, sealed unit suspensions and pneumatic throttles were too clever and had to be revised. Against the background of Rootes Group difficulties and take-over by Chrysler the projected production figure of 150,000 was wildly optimistic. From a peak of nearly 70,000 in 1964, production quickly settled down to around 44,000 before the Imp fizzled out in 1976, undeveloped and largely unloved.

X FACTOR

The last complete project for Issigonis was the 9X, a remarkable 6in (152mm) shorter but 2in (51mm) wider than the Mini. The suspension was conventional; at the front were MacPherson struts with trailing arms and coil springs. Power plants were overhead cam units developed by Downton Engineering with four or six cylinders allied to a hydrostatic transmission, a forerunner of the constantly variable transmissions of the 1980s.

Best of all, the body style incorporated a tailgate. Hatchbacks may be common now, but this was a novelty then, especially on such a small car. Researching through Issigonis files from this era I came across a very detailed MIRA vehicle analysis on the 1965 Autobianchi Primula. This Fiat based car not only bore a strong physical resemblance to the 9X but had a front-wheel-drive layout and a tailgate. Clearly Issigonis had been strongly influenced by the Italian design.

Despite the existence of the Autobianchi, a marque little known outside Italy, the supermini had been born in the shape of the 9X and it was ready for approval in 1968. However, the new BLMC management knew how little money the original Mini

was making and did not want to make the same mistake. Even so the *BLMC Volume Passenger Division Proposal for a new 750–1000cc Mini* dated 9 August 1968 was very focused: 'The objective is to provide a car with room for four adults and some luggage, within a competitive specification, at a price 5% below the current Mini, with the aim of major penetration into the world small car market, particularly in Europe.'

The proposal went on: 'Briefly it comprises a new body shell 6in shorter and 2.5in wider than the current Mini, but with the interior dimensions identical. The engine is a completely new 4 cylinder, with a maximum design capacity of 1000cc. Initially it would be offered in 750cc and 950cc forms opening up to 850cc and 1000cc two years after introduction. Six-cylinder versions of 1200/1500cc can be developed of completely new design. The engine weight is 40% less than the current A series and it has a considerably narrower silhouette. Basic design is single overhead camshaft. Double OHC heads with hemispherical chambers are being developed.' Then there was a projection that would come

The 9X from 1969 with its radical hatchback styling could have been the supermini quantum leap that Issigonis and British Leyland were looking for. Unfortunately they could not afford it.

to haunt the Metro: 'Predicted production 360,000, 120,000 more than Mini with an 8 year design life. Introduction for the October 1971 Motor Show.' None of those things happened, but the production forecast was used to justify a huge investment for the Metro a decade later. At the time, though, the product planning department was very enthusiastic about the 9X and wrote: 'It is recommended that this programme be authorized at the earliest possible date.'

Clearly Issigonis had proposed another truly innovative small car, so not surprisingly he was very bitter about the cancellation. Apparently he modified his views once the 'me too' Euroboxes arrived in the 1970s when the 9X would have been indistinguishable. Surely the point would have been that the 9X was unique and hard to beat. Priced properly it could have made up for all those early losses and proved that a mini car could make a maxi profit. Sadly, another opportunity had been missed.

FRONT-WHEEL-DRIVE FAMILY

BMC announced what was effectively the Mini's successor: the Austin/Morris 1100. This family saloon styled by Pininfarina came with the revolutionary Hydrolastic suspension system. Roomy and economical, only the small boot counted against it. Nevertheless, between 1963 and 1971 it was Britain's best selling car. Not chic, or a motorsport natural, it was a safe and sensible car with a very wide appeal. Once again, BMC messed up the pricing. At £592 the sophisticated 1100 cost just £1 more than the conventional Ford Cortina. The 1100 showed up BMC's poor product planning as it sold against the Morris Minor and Austin A40, which shared the 1,098cc A series engine.

What the 1100 did do was to set a design philosophy whereby the Corporation aimed to produce technically advanced cars that would enjoy long production runs and not incur large re-tooling costs. The Mini concept was stretched even further when in October 1964 the 1800 model was launched. This was a big car, which was even bigger on the inside; all the space utilization lessons learnt on the Mini and 1100 were employed to roomy effect on this transverse engined, front-wheel-drive saloon. The execution, however, was less than successful. The styling was an unhappy combination of Issigonis and Pininfarina, with the Mini designer taking care of the centre section while Sergio Farina styled the front end. According to Issigonis the Italian copied the Fiat headlamps, 'which were the worst feature of the car.'

The problem with the 1800 was that big cars are traditionally conservative in both styling and innovation; the novelty of a remarkable amount of practical and usable space was lost on most buyers. Structurally it was one of the strongest monocoque hulls ever built, but the 1800 and its successors were always unkindly referred to as 'Landcrabs'. Issigonis, though, always rated the 1800: 'I still think it was our best car. I loved that car.'

Less lovable was the Austin Maxi, intended to slot between the 1100 and 1800. A lot of money had been spent on development by the time BLMC was formed and the decision was made to press ahead with production. Launched in April 1969, the hatchback styling should have been a sensation, but it looked a little dull. The new E series engine was flawed as was the five-speed gearbox. It was a missed opportunity; when these problems were finally sorted out it sold a consistent 30,000 units a year until 1981.

Equally disastrous was the Allegro, launched in May 1973. This was meant to replace the 1100/1300, which was still sell-ing strongly into the 1970s. It had a bigger boot and similar interior room, but was a larger car overall. Worst of all, the styling was blobby and bland. Its best sales were in 1975 at 63,339, which was half what the 1100/1300 achieved at its peak.

The front-wheel-drive strategy should have worked. BLMC should have ruth-lessly rationalized the range, re-priced the models and as John Barber proposed at the time, reposition the company. 'We could have moved Austin and Morris grad-ually up market; that would have kept vol-ume down. It would not have been a sud-den change but each successive car would

have been more expensive than its prede-cessor ... We decided, in due course, that we would adopt the BMW/Mercedes-Benz approach rather than the Ford one. But we didn't have a hope in hell. We had too may different models made in too many differ-ent places.'

In view of BMW's acquisition of Rover these were prophetic words. It is clear to see where any potential development money went, squandered around the group rather than forging a new identity and innovative models. Meanwhile, the great grandfather of British front wheel drive – the Mark II Mini –soldiered on, notching up bigger sales figures than ever.

The Mini spawned a generation of front-wheel-drive cars and outlived them all. Of all the Mini spin-offs, the 1100/1300 range was most successful.

4   1970s Revival – The Mark III

*'Everyone stopped buying expensive cars
in order to buy the ruddy Mini again.'*

Lord Stokes – *Wheels of Misfortune*

'ADO 20' is not a very romantic model nomen-
clature. Why not call it simply the Mini? So
they did, or more precisely BLMC did. To
coincide with a number of important changes,
the slate was wiped clean and from October
1969 the Mini was reborn and renamed.

The Mini's parent company had gone
through a name change crisis all its own,
and BLMC now consolidated all the independent British car manufacturers: Austin,
Morris, Jaguar, Rover and Triumph. Ratio-
nalization became the name of the game as

*Spot the difference: wind-up windows, new Mini badge and fixed door handles. This is an 850cc at its
most basic – minimal bright work, no heater and just the one sun visor.*

the company saw that badge engineering was marginalizing and confusing customers. A single brand image was needed to market the car more effectively. No one really bought cars out of loyalty, only on performance, price and practicality – a tough lesson that BLMC learnt fully only when the Japanese invasion was in full mid-1970s swing. For the moment, though, the company was gearing up for one of the most successful periods in the life of the Mini.

NEW MINI?

A glance at the new Mini Mark III involved a double take. Initially it did not look that different from the previous incarnation, despite simple Mini badging and blue Leyland postage stamp emblems on the A panels. In fact, the whole body shell had been comprehensively re-jigged. The floor pan had been revised, along with the boot floor, windscreen surround, front parcel shelf and bonnet hinges. More obviously, those external door hinges had finally been replaced by enclosed ones, which cleaned up the side of the car nicely. The doors were the focus of the most attention as they were now slightly larger and incorporated wind-up window mechanisms from the Elf and Hornet. In practical terms that meant a very large 5in (127mm) reduction in interior width and sacrificing the cavernous door pockets. Many lamented the fact that the Mini was going soft and was not so spartan anymore. Even the hinged rear number plate was bolted firmly to the boot lid in a deeper recess in recognition of the fact that few owners would bother to overload the inadequate boot.

Under the skin was a fundamental rethink on the suspension front, with a return to the dry rubber-cone system first used in 1959. Some drivers found it a little bouncy, but generally the Hydrolastic system worked

well enough; unfortunately, the system was expensive to manufacture. Other uprates included negative Earth electrics and a mechanical fuel pump.

AS ISSIGONIS INTENDED – 850 (1969–80)

On the model line-up front, the basic 850 remained just that. Single instrument, fixed rear quarter windows, optional heater and just the one visor, so if you still wanted to buy a spartan runabout in 1969, this was it, with no comfortable Super De Luxe alternative. Even the direct change and magic wand gear lever remained. Buyers could spoil themselves by specifying an automatic gearbox, but only until 1971.

In 1974 the 850 almost became luxurious. Never mind the inertia reel seat belts, a fresh air heater was finally standard along with a heated rear window, a second sun visor for the passenger and a driver's door mirror. The general uprating of the 850 continued apace in the mid 1970s: it got new seats and vinyl covers in 1975 complete with anti-tip catches and revised door pocket trim.

Then there was a major interior facelift in 1976 as the instrumentation was uprated. The console now had rocker switches (hazards, heated rear window, brake circuit failure test, lights and heater controller plus the choke). At the driver's feet were larger pedals donated from the Allegro. Owners still wrestled with a bus-sized steering wheel, but there was a new ignition lock on the column and two control stalks. By 1977 there were even a vanity mirror, padded steering wheel and a handbrake grip that had also first seen service in the Allegro.

Apart from the cosmetics there were subtle range changes that made the Mini more driveable: improved synchromesh, an alternator and remote gear change in 1972, radial ply

Mini 850 (October 1969 to August 1980)

Engine

Type	Four cylinder in line; cast iron block transversely mounted in front
Capacity	848cc
Bore and stroke	62.94mm × 68.3mm
Output	34bhp at 5,500rpm; 37bhp at 5,500rpm from June 1974; automatic 39bhp at 5,250
Compression ratio	8.3:1; automatic 9.0:1
Maximum torque	44lb.ft at 2,900rpm; 43lb.ft at 2,800rpm from June 1974; automatic 44.8lb.ft at 2,500rpm

Transmission

Type	Front-wheel drive
Gear ratios	4-speed 3.765/5.317/8.176/13.657 13.657 (reverse) (final drive)
	4-speed automatic

Suspension

Front	Wishbones, rubber cones, telescopic dampers
Rear	Trailing arms, rubber cones, telescopic dampers
Steering	Rack and pinion

Brakes Hydraulic drum/drum

Tyres/Wheels 5.2in × 10in cross-ply/3.5in × 10in

Dimensions

Track (front)	47.375in (1,203mm)
Track (rear)	45.875in (1,165mm)
Wheelbase	80.2in (2,037mm)
Length	120.25in (3,054mm)
Width	55.5in (1,410mm)
Height	53in (1,346mm)
Unladen weight	1,360lb (617kg)
Fuel capacity	5.5 gallons (25 litres)

Performance

Top speed	77mph (124kph)
Acceleration	0–60mph in 20.3 seconds
Fuel consumption	38mpg (7.4 litres per 100km)

Purchase price £596

Production 407,600

tyres a year later. For 1974 a new carburettor, revised manifolds, air cleaner and twin silencer exhaust made a difference, followed by softened rear suspension in 1976. On the outside there were few changes; only a matt black grille in 1977 made a real difference.

Although the 850 slipped quietly from the price lists in 1980 just as the Mini Metro arrived, there were a couple of swan song models at the two extremes of the specification spectrum. In 1979 the City embraced the original Austin Se7en's Spartan specification with colour keyed black bumpers, roof gutter, wheel arches and City decal on each front wing and the boot complete with a three band coachline. Inside, there was dogstooth check upholstery. The antidote to that poverty specification model was a Super De Luxe. It mirrored the 1000, which meant three-instrument binnacle, striped seats, fitted carpets and decent roll ball ventilation. In the 850's last year it even benefited from the last few range uprates over the closing months. So a 7.5 gallon (34 litre) fuel tank boosted the range and much trumpeted sound deadening made those longer journeys even quieter.

MINI 1000

The Mini 1000 took over from where the Mark II Super De Luxe left off: better trim, opening rear windows, heater, two sun visors, three-instrument binnacle and full width wheel trims. Most of the mechanical changes were as the 850, although the trim was repeatedly uprated: better carpets in 1974, eyeball fresh air vents in 1976 and from 1977 reclining seats. These new seats were covered in two-tone nylon. Everyone now knew that the Mini was backing in their direction as reversing lights were standard. Door map pockets at the front came in useful as did the dipping rear view mirror.

Car Magazine were not that impressed by the Mini 1000 when they tested it in February 1975 as a response to the rapidly rising price of petrol and citing the fact that 40mpg (7l/100km) would be the minimum acceptable consumption figure for the contemporary car. They pitched the Mini against a Fiat 127 and Toyota 1000. 'The elaborate fittings of the Toyota are attractive, and so is its smooth, happy engine, but it falls down by being short on interior space and having only mediocre

By the late 1970s, the Mini had undergone minor changes, for example the black grille, but it is still essentially the 1959 design.

Mini 1,000cc (October 1969 to April 1982)

Engine

Type	Four cylinder in line; cast iron block transversely mounted in front
Capacity	998cc
Bore and stroke	64.6 × 76.2mm
Output	38bhp at 5,250rpm; 40bhp at 5,100rpm from June 1974; automatic 41bhp at 4,850
Compression ratio	8.3:1; automatic 8.9:1
Maximum torque	52lb.ft at 2,700rpm; 51lb.ft at 2,600 from June 1974; automatic 52lb.ft at 2,750rpm

Transmission

Type	Front-wheel drive
Gear ratios	4-speed 3.765/5.317/8.176/13.657 13.657 (reverse) (final drive) 4-speed automatic

Suspension

Front	Wishbones, rubber cones, telescopic dampers
Rear	Trailing arms, rubber cones, telescopic dampers
Steering	Rack and pinion

Brakes   Hydraulic drum/drum

Tyres/Wheels   5.2in × 10in cross-ply/3.5in × 10in

Dimensions

Track (front)	47.375in (1,203mm)
Track (rear)	45.875in (1,165mm)
Wheelbase	80.2in (2,037mm)
Length	120.25in (3,054mm)
Width	55.5in (1,410mm)
Height	53in (1,346mm)
Unladen weight	1,400lb (635kg)
Fuel capacity	5.5 gallons (25 litres)

Performance

Top speed	82mph (132kph)
Acceleration	0–60mph in 18.7 seconds
Fuel consumption,	38.8mpg (35.3 litres per 100km); automatic 40.2mpg (141.3 litres per 100km)

Purchase price   £675

Production   1,439,819

Mini City, from 1979 the most basic form of Mini motoring with eye-catching decals and even luxurious dogstooth cloth trim on the inside. Otherwise it was poverty specification all the way with matt black bumpers, and the traditional single instrument binnacle.

handling and road holding … The Mini is an embarrassment. It is painfully out of date in just about every respect except price, but will continue to find adherents regardless; it may not be a good car any more, but it is a convenient one that the vast majority of people understand … Of course the Fiat is by far the best value. The very fact that its interior can be converted into a sort of estate car is a tremendous point in its favour.'

Despite criticism the Mini not only stayed in production, but prospered. As the car reached its 20th birthday, *Autocar* celebrated with a fairly positive road test in August 1979 and came up with some useful explanations as to why the Mini had survived. 'It is not in the least surprising to hear recently that Mini sales were shooting up again. A car like this, which offers a near certain 40mpg to the normal owner – provided he or she does not drive flat out all of the time – is vital to many pockets these days … On the open road, the limitations of the performance become more obvious … Those who appreciate the cardinal virtues of driving – good steering, road holding, responsiveness, stability are the ones that apply here – have confessed at one time or another to an unavoidable affection for the Mini … The immediate unthinking reaction today on some people's part is that the Mini

Mini insects

Three Mini replacements were seriously considered in 1972 and were given insect project names. There was the Ant, a dimensionally identical car to the Mini, which although it reached the clay model stage was deemed too close to the original to be worth developing. Then there was the Dragonfly (a name that was surfacing yet again in the Mini's history), a booted saloon that was rejected fairly quickly. Finally the Ladybird, which was 18in (457mm) longer than the Mini and featured a hatchback rear, received approval quite rapidly. Codenamed ADO 74, it went from clay model to full-size buck in record time.

Harris Mann, stylist of the Allegro, TR7 and Princess, was briefed to come up with a larger and more profitable model and at 138in (3,505mm) by 61.5in (1,562mm) it was just that. Its £130 million development mirrored the work being done at Ford on the Fiesta and the ADO 74 could have been launched at the same time. It even had MacPherson strut suspension, and could have featured an early version of the remarkable K series engine, which later went on to power the Rover Metro. Another victim of market research, ADO 74 was killed off for not being distinctive, or a direct Mini replacement.

has been overtaken by the competition. This is only half true – for the simple reason that torpedoes most of the argument right at the start, that the Mini has few competitors. Such critics are thinking of Fiat's 127, Renault's 5, Volkswagen's Polo or Ford's Fiesta – but these are all very much bigger cars. Of the ten breeds of under one litre car which in any way compete with the Mini, none are much over 10 feet long – the Fiat 126 is the nearest at 10ft 3in – and the rest are none less than a foot longer; and of those only four have appreciably better overall inside space. If you really want the minimum of car there isn't much other than the Mini.'

Minissima, perhaps one of the most innovative Mini re-skins. The side facing, and perhaps slightly cramped, rear seat can be seen.

MINISSIMA

Designer William Towns, famous for styling the Aston Martin DB6, made a big impact at the 1973 London Motor Show. Incredibly his model was even smaller than the Mini at a stunted 90in (2,286mm) long. The track, height and width were all identical on this motorized cube, which was powered by a Mini engine and automatic gearbox. There was just one door, at the back, and the idea was that it could park at right angles to the kerb so that everyone could exit safely from the rear. There was conventional seating up front, while those at the back sat opposite each other. It was such an interesting concept that BL bought the rights, used it as a promotional vehicle and then stuck it in the Heritage Museum. It was an interesting concept and should have been developed.

MINI? METRO? – ADO 88

BLMC ceased to exist on 27 June 1975 when it was renamed British Leyland Ltd (BL). The company had been nationalized after a steady slide towards insolvency. Sir Don Ryder had been commissioned to make a report about the state of the company and recommended that BL should stay as a producer of volume and specialist cars aided by huge injections of public money. Perhaps the most damaging recommendation was amalgamating all the car divisions into one. It did not work, and BL lurched to another cash crisis in 1977. Ford became the nation's biggest builder of cars, largely by importing hundreds of thousands from its plants in Europe. As Michael Edwardes took over as BL Chairman it all looked pretty bleak with staff problems, plant closures and an incoherent model policy.

Probably the bleakest thing on the horizon was ADO 88, the Mini's replacement. It was BL's most advanced new project, having cost £300m to develop, yet within a couple of months Edwardes had canned it. He was quoted as saying that the car had looked like turning into a national disaster. Customer clinics were held around Britain and Europe and on one occasion a mere 3 per cent of the 500 questioned expressed a preference for the proposed new Mini, whereas 40 per cent responded very favourably to the all-new Ford Fiesta. Part of the problem may have been that the ADO 88 was not the radical quantum leap that the original Mini had been.

ADO 88 had been due to make its debut at the first motor show to be held at the National Exhibition Centre in Birmingham in 1978. In overall charge of the project was Technical Director Charles Griffin, who was aiming to address the old Mini's shortcomings of too much noise and not enough refinement while boosting the interior space by making it

bigger. Harris Mann did the styling and there was a hint of Princess 'wedge' about it all. The length was 126in (3,200mm), the track at the rear was now the same as the front and an extra 2in (51mm) width was accommodated by curved body sides. Mechanically there did not seem to be any power unit better suited to the job than the old A series. So a £30m programme to update it as the A plus was initiated. Like the original Mini the suspension was to be a crucial factor in the car's success. To keep the interior packaging neat and the floor usefully flat, Hydragas suspension, as later used on the Metro, was proposed.

However, the bodywork seemed to be the big problem area. Pininfarina were even asked to chip in with their interpretation on the small hatchback theme in 1976, which was deemed just too pretentious. In the cold light of the Europe-wide customer clinics the reaction was far from favourable. The decision was taken to upgrade the model to supermini specification and dimensions if it was to stand any chance against the Fiesta, Volkswagen Polo or Fiat 127. The new project was codenamed LC8, but underpinning it all was ADO 88.

Market research indicated that the new car would not immediately replace the Mini. It was still useful to BL dealers as a second car proposition for two-car families. So the Mini was saved yet again. In June 1979 ADO 88 became the Metro after a ballot of the workforce put that name ahead of 'Maestro'.

MINIOMICS 3 – 1970s BOOM

The Mini entered the 1970s in very rude health as the unassailable small car. The absolute peak was reached in 1971 as combined production of Minis and Clubmans topped 320,000. It was the fourth best selling car in 1970, moved up to second behind the

1100/1300 a year later then sixth in 1972, fifth in 1973 rising to third a year later and even entered the 1980s in fourth spot. Although the Mini missed the Suez crisis fuel restriction measures that inspired it, it was in the right place at the right time in 1973.

First, there was the Arab–Israeli War, which seriously affected Britain's oil supplies; the price quadrupled. To counter the effects the Conservative government introduced the three-day working week from January 1974 and imposed a national 50mph (80kph) speed limit. Trade union opposition to the government's counter-inflation measures resulted in the miners' strike. Not surprisingly the car that the nervous, frightened and frugal buyer turned to was the Mini. Much to British Leyland's annoyance the loss-making Mini overtook the relatively new Morris Marina as their top seller for 1974. The same thing happened again in 1979 when petrol prices soared after the

Iranian revolution. The marginally profitable Mini led the way for BL, with the Marina and Allegro bringing up the rear.

The Mini was clearly the car you bought in a crisis – the model that you could rely on to be economical, reliable and practical. It appeared to be irreplaceable. However, the era of the supermini was dawning. After being unchallenged for so long, with just a few irritating imports to deal with, the biggest threat was to come from within. Ford, who had previously avoided the small car market, came up with their own interpretation: the Fiesta. This hatchback, announced in July 1976 and costing one billion dollars to develop, finally overhauled the Mini's sales figures in 1980 shifting 91,661 compared to the Mini's 61,129, still pretty impressive for a 21-year-old.

British Leyland had to do something. That something was the Metro, but that was a different model and another decade.

The extended Mini family pictured at the Mini Exhibition in July 1980. (Back row, left to right) Mini based MG ADO 34, Monte Carlo winning Cooper S, Outspan Orange promotional vehicle, customized Mini called Li'l Dream, Crayford Hornet Convertible; (middle row) ADO 70 prototype, Unipower GT, Twinnie Moke, Marcos, Crompton Leyland Electricar; (front row) Morris Mini Minor, Morris Mini Minor sectioned and a contemporary 1980 Mini.

5 Still Going Strong – 1980s and 1990s

'Today the Mini's virtues of compactness and economy are as relevant as they ever were.'

Autocar

As the Mini entered yet another decade it had a new rival to contend with. This new small car came from the same organization, so they had plenty in common, not least the ancient A series engine. For a while they even shared a name; though officially referred to as just 'Metro', for the first couple of years the car was generically a 'Mini Metro' to the great British public. With the Metro's hatchback, Eurobox styling, purpose built, robot-operated factory and huge marketing push the Mini's days had to be numbered.

However, although market research revealed to British Leyland that the Mini should stay in production, the intention was still to replace it by the early 1980s. Michael Edwardes had envisaged a product-led recovery that meant direct replacements for the Allegro and Marina as well, but this could hardly happen overnight. When they finally arrived, the Maestro and Montego were not worth the wait. In fact, there had always been a curious reliance by BL and BMC on the loyalty of private UK customers. Time and again these regimes failed to make any conquest sales by snatching customers away from the likes of Vauxhall and Ford with a better product. All that seemed to happen was that the new model ended up selling in the same quantities as its predecessor.

METRONOMICS

The root of the problem with the new Metro, an otherwise competent addition to super-mini league, was the wildly over optimistic predictions for sales. Edwardes may have initiated the styling rethink, but sales forecasts remained the same. The BL board simply did not consider the impact of competing with the new superminis in the marketplace, like the Fiesta and Polo, which would inevitably end up pinching sales from the Metro. The original sales estimates from the late 1960s related to the prototype 9X and predicted a minimum of 350,000 units, yet the Metro never sold even half that figure. The Mini was being produced at a rate of 200,000 between 1975 and 1978, but those volumes were reduced dramatically to make way for its replacement. By 1982 worldwide sales of Minis ran at 52,000, while the Metro chalked up 174,000 units at its peak. This meant that BL made no increase in small car sales and had in fact started to lose out as volumes of both cars started to plummet as the 1980s wore on.

The Mini entered a new decade as a neglected model with a loyal following; after all this time it was now proving to be profitable. Any changes were forced by emissions

Metro, the Mini's replacement. Except it was not.

or safety legislation, and sales were stimulated by special editions. For the Mini enthusiast the situation was far from perfect, but at least their favourite car was surviving and, by the 1990s, even starting to prosper.

THE LAST MINI? – 1000

The imminent arrival of its close relative and rival, the Metro, triggered a number of changes in advance of that launch, which would also see a large number of common parts shared around the range. In October 1979 the 1000 was renamed the Super. With the passing of the basic 850 the City name was now transferred to the 1000 model in September 1980 with a similarly poverty-stricken specification. At that time the Super was re-badged 1000 HL, a designation used liberally throughout the British Leyland empire to signify a 'high line' level of specification.

With the Mini, the HL signalled a whole host of changes from the purely cosmetic adoption of the Clubman interior to Metro running gear. So out went the old centrally mounted binnacle and in came a Tupperware box-like double instrument pod. In addition there was tinted glass, larger door bins and a Metro steering wheel, gear knob and window winders. Under the bonnet was the Metro's A-plus engine and gearbox. On top of the bonnet was a new Mini badge fitted to the saloons incorporating a cross of St George mounted on the usual shield, while in the middle of the grille was the Austin Morris corporate logo. Unofficially, models built from this point onwards are regarded as Mark IV Minis, even though some pedants might argue that the changes in 1984 were a touch more radical in pure watershed terms.

Motor magazine also took the Mini's side after trying the new 1000HL in July 1981. 'The best things about a Mini are still, in 1981, at least as good as they ever were. Its combination of diminutive dimensions, panoramic visibility, eager engine, snappy gear change and scampering manoeuvrability still make it a cheekily effective town car which is great fun to drive … and in its latest form we see no reason why it shouldn't continue to feature in the best-sellers list for years to come.'

The 1980 Mini 1000.

DISCS, BIG WHEELS, ECONOMY

For 1982 the emphasis was on economy. There was re-designation all round as the City E and HLE models featured 2.95:1 final drives and high compression cylinder heads. Upmarket minis were repositioned and renamed as the Mayfair in October with significant trim improvements including Raschelle velour upholstery, pile carpets, tinted glass, radio, passenger door mirror, head restraints and locking petrol cap. By 1984 the Mini caught up with braking technology by fitting front disc brakes. It seems incredible this was not done earlier in view of the specially made Cooper discs in 1961, which were small but very effective for the time. This development was also joined by 12in wheels, and surrounding them wider arches.

In 1985 the City E finally got decent air ventilation, courtesy of the corner mounted swivelling eyeball vents that had been available since 1969. One of the most enduring interior features had been the single central instrument binnacle, but even that was replaced by the two dial pod. A four-spoke steering wheel and revised stalk made control easier. On the outside the all important City logo was shifted to the rear three quarter panel and there were new wheel trims.

The Mayfair also benefited from several changes. Inside, the instrument binnacle now had a rev counter, which was framed by a three-spoke steering wheel, new gear knob, revised trim and on the outside full width wheel trims. Both models gained side indicators on the front wings and there was some new branding on the grille, which bore the legend 'Austin' above the corporate logo.

Mini 1,000cc (April 1982 to May 1992)

Engine

Type	Four cylinder in line; cast iron block transversely mounted in front
Capacity	998cc
Bore and stroke	64.6 × 76.2mm
Output	40bhp at 5,000rpm; automatic 41bhp at 4,850rpm
Compression ratio	10.3:1; automatic 8.9:1
Maximum torque	50lb.ft at 2,500rpm; automatic 52lb.ft at 2,750rpm

Transmission

Type	Front-wheel drive
Gear ratios	4-speed 2.95/4.23/6.54/10.43
	4-speed automatic (as above)

Suspension

Front	Independent, wishbones with rubber cones and telescopic dampers
Rear	Independent trailing arms with rubber cones and telescopic dampers
Steering	Rack and pinion

Brakes

Hydraulic drum/drum; front discs from October 1984; servo from October 1988

Tyres/Wheels

3.5in × 10in/12in; 145 SR–12 from 1984

Dimensions

Track (front)	47.375in (1,203mm)
Track (rear)	45.875in (1,165mm)
Wheelbase	80.2in (2,037mm)
Length	120.25in (3,054mm)
Width	55.5in (1,410mm)
Height	53in (1,346mm); 53.25in (1,353mm) from October 1984
Unladen weight	Mayfair 1,420lb (644kg)
	City 1,380lb (626kg)
Luggage capacity	4.1cu ft (116 litres)
Fuel capacity	7.5 gallons (34 litres)

Performance

Top speed	82mph (132kph)
Acceleration	0–60mph in 17.9 seconds
Fuel consumption	45.9mpg (31.4 litres per 100km); automatic 40.9mpg (31.4 litres per 100km)

Purchase price

From	£2,999

Production

Since 1969	1,439,800

The upmarket Mini Mayfair, with luxury touches on the inside. The fancy plastic wheel trims, coachline, decals and passenger door mirror set it apart from the City.

Improved Mayfair interior with a triple instrument binnacle, three-spoke steering wheel and new cloth on the seats.

The revised Mini City with 12in wheels, disc brakes, and economy 'E' engine.

Radically altered interior for the base City with air vents and a double instrument binnacle.

True to form, that name lasted only until 1987 when a new 'Mini' badge took pride of place on the bonnet.

MINI REVIEWED

Autocar tested the revised Mini in 1985 and compared it with five cars similarly priced but significantly larger, in the shape of the Skoda Estelle 105S, Lada Riva 1200L, Yugo 45, Fiat Panda 45CL and Citröen 2CV Charleston. 'Twenty-five years after its launch, the Mini is selling 23,000 cars a year comfortably ahead of any other in its class. Why? Probably because today the Mini's virtues of compactness and economy are as relevant as they ever were. The Mini is to the small car what Hoover is to the vacuum cleaner and Kodak is to cameras … The Mini is the least powerful car in this group, but with an unladen weight of 11.9cwt it is easily the lightest. Thus it has respectable performance which is not far short of the newer Panda … with a wheel at each corner and minimum suspension travel, the Mini is but one step removed from a go-kart and feels it. In sheer handling agility the Mini makes the other cars in this group seem positively leviathan by comparison … Above all, it is still fun.'

ISSIGONIS – THE TWILIGHT YEARS

Official recognition for Issigonis came with a CBE (Commander of the British Empire) in 1964, followed by a well deserved knighthood in 1969. However, his influence ended with the creation of BLMC. Key posts were allocated elsewhere, but he never stopped working, eventually being retained as a design consultant for Austin Rover until his death in October 1988. But

BL turns Rover

In 1986 BL reported losses of £892 million. The Government insisted on new management and a new Chairman; the man chosen was Graham Day, a tall Canadian lawyer who had been running the nationalized British Shipbuilders. By 1987 Day had disposed of some corporate assets and the company recorded a £27.9 million pre-tax profit. Then in 1988 British Aerospace bought the renamed Rover Group.

Meanwhile, the Mini's future was being seriously debated and in 1986 the idea of dropping the car was being seriously considered. Of course, Day was inundated with protest letters when the news leaked out. The development route that the company chose initially was the special edition syndrome.

did they consult? Unfortunately not, and Sir Alec was disappointed that none of his suggested refinements were ever adopted. He never stopped building advanced Mini-based prototypes.

A favourite was the gearless Mini, which had a long stroke big torque engine driving through a hydraulic torque converter. While Michael Edwardes was in charge, Issigonis lent an example to the BL chief for commuting around London, but nothing came of this interesting concoction of his ideas. The overhead camshaft engine was that developed for the hatchback 9X. The suspension was almost conventional, featuring coil springs, which increased roll but did not hamper the car's overall nimbleness. When Richard Bremner drove the car in 1989 he commented, 'Amusingly, this Mini was converted by Issigonis to have sliding windows and door pockets, despite the fact that it was made well after these features were ditched.' As to the concept, 'The advantages are certainly strong – spectacularly reduced cost, reduced noise, a vastly more compact powertrain, less complication, and less work for the driver.'

Issigonis also spent time developing innovative power plants for Minis, including a steam unit, a 1,500cc diesel and a 1,100cc six-cylinder engine. Talking to old friend Ronald Barker, Issigonis outlined his new Mini car philosophy, 'We're looking for refinement, not power, and in this respect the difference between the four and six [cylinder] is dramatic. The small car of today is screaming for refinement, less road noise as well as less mechanical noise, because it's a complete waste of time to have one without the other.'

Issigonis was not just a design genius. He was single-minded, obstinate and egotistical – traits that Donald Stokes loathed, but which explained the keys to his success and eccentricities. A preference for sliding windows over wind-ups and a ban on radios only added to his mystique. Issigonis knew that the Mini was a one-off and this quote

serves as an epitaph and a warning to all manufacturers, 'If one pioneers something, and it is not copied, then it is a failure … Small cars are so boring, they are ghastly, they all look the same because they are designed by committees trying to copy the Mini.'

NO MORE 998

The 998cc engine's time was limited as the 'E' tag was dropped in 1988 and it became the simple City again. Head restraints and a three-spoke steering wheel made a significant difference inside and there was even an extra 1bhp under the bonnet. Mayfair models now had radio cassettes and minor trim changes to tempt buyers. A standard brake servo certainly made them safer in 1988 and an optional catalytic converter a year later meant that they could be fashionably green too. In spite of this, the most ancient A series power units had to die, but not before some

Issigonis retires from BL in 1972 and is pictured with his finest creations from Morris Minors (out of shot) to an 1800, one of his favourites. He remained as a consultant to BL and Rover until his death in 1988.

serious marketing attention had been turned to the run out models. On the City this meant full width wheel trims, a return to chrome bumpers and snazzy harlequin trim. The Mayfair also got the glamour treatment with a chrome-effect grille, chrome Mayfair badge on the boot, colour keyed door mirrors and number plate lamp.

THE 1,275 ENGINE FOR 1992

When the Metro got the K series engine in 1990, pundits wondered why the Mini did not get the transplant to give the car a new lease of life and meet stringent emission regulations. The official reason was that it would not fit and even if they re-engineered the engine bay, the car would fail the strict European type approval regulations. So in June 1992 the Mini entered an important new phase of production. Powering the new version, unofficially known as the Mark V, was a 50bhp three-way catalysed version of the 1,275cc engine last seen in the Metro.

Replacing the City as the entry level Mini was the Sprite, a late model City re-run complete with full width wheel trims,

chrome bumpers, chrome Mini badge, Sprite decals on the rear side panel and harlequin trim inside. The new Mayfair also mirrored the old 998cc model with chrome effect grille, colour keyed door mirrors and chrome finish on the Mini and Mayfair badges. Inside, there was chevron decorated velour trim. Outside, the wheel trims were identical to the Sprite's, although Minilite style alloys as seen on the Cooper could be ordered as an option.

BMiniW

The Mayfair received a major interior facelift in March 1993, when a full width burr walnut dashboard was fixed into place. For years customizers had been inserting their own planks of wood into the fascia and finally Rover had decided to do the same. Maybe they had forgotten that the Riley Elf had featured such a fascia and that came with two glove boxes. Three dials were mounted on a slightly proud section, while the radio sat mid dash with an analogue clock above it and in front of the passenger was the novelty of an opening glove box. Both the Sprite and Mayfair also benefited

Inside the new Mayfair, with for the first time a full width burr walnut dashboard, incorporating a glove box, radio cassette and clock, plus front seats from the Metro.

Mini Sprite and Mayfair (May 1992 to October 1996)

Engine

Type	Four cylinder in line; cast iron block transversely mounted in front
Capacity	1,275cc
Bore and stroke	70.64 × 81.33mm
Output	50bhp at 5,000rpm
Compression ratio	10.5:1
Maximum torque	66lb.ft at 2,600rpm

Transmission

Type	Front-wheel drive
Gear ratios	4-speed 3.11/4.43/6.79/11.34/(reverse) 11.40
	4-speed automatic 3.76/5.49/6.94/10.11

Suspension

Front	Independent, wishbones with rubber cones and telescopic dampers
Rear	Independent trailing arms with rubber cones and telescopic dampers
Steering	Rack and pinion

Brakes   Disc/drum

Tyres/Wheels   12 × 4.5in steel 145/70 SR–12 radial ply

Dimensions

Track (front)	48.8in (1,240mm)
Track (rear)	47.6in (1,209mm)
Wheelbase	80.1in (2,035mm)
Length	120.25in (3,054mm)
Width	55.5in (1,410mm)
Height	53.25 (1,353mm)
Unladen weight	1,375lb (624kg)
Luggage capacity	4.1cu ft (116 litres)
Fuel capacity	7.5 gallons (34 litres)

Performance

Top speed	87mph (140kph); automatic 82mph (132kph)
Acceleration	0–60mph in 13.4 seconds
Fuel consumption	37.3mpg (94.2 litres per 100km); automatic 35.5mpg (56.5 litres per 100km)

Purchase price

Sprite	£5,753
Mayfair	£6,932

A 1993 model Mayfair, with 1,275cc fuel injected power and optional alloys.

from larger front Metro seats, re-styled door bins, a boot mat, new badging and remarkably, after all this time, an internal bonnet release. Other security measures included a visible vehicle identification number etched onto the glass and an alarm and immobilizer fitted as standard to Mayfairs.

As Mayfairs went further up-market, the company that sold it went on the market. Controversially on 31 January 1994, British Aerospace were reported to be selling Rover to BMW for £800 million. The history of the motor industry in Britain took another twist, but the Mini was in safe hands, not least because the BMW Chairman was a distant relative of Issigonis who fully appreciated the importance of this marvellous little car.

Sprites got a little brighter in June 1995 when a chrome lock set (door handles and boot release) was fitted. Inside, new fabric trim was topped off with a black carpet and a radio cassette with a removable front panel.

MINI VERSUS THE REST

The Mini was rarely matched against its rivals in the 1980s and 1990s, mainly because there were no rivals. In fact, pint-sized contemporaries of the original 1959 Mini were pretty thin on the ground after thirty years. There was the Trabant (1958–90), a hideous two-stroke, always well past its sell-by date as underneath the ugly plastic body was a pre-war DKW. After the Berlin wall fell, Volkswagen bought the business and tried to keep the Trabbie going by installing a Polo power plant. It fooled no one.

The NSU Prinz (1958–73) from the Western side of the Wall was the most civilized and initially cramped alternative to the Mini. The re-skinned Prinz 4 and alloy engined 1000 were worthy rivals, but the rear engine layout was always a problem. The same goes for the Volkswagen Beetle (1945 to date), not really a direct competitor in terms of size, but as a people's car – the sort that motorized nations – it compares. Full of character but slow, large yet cramped, it never got near victory in the Monte Carlo Rally, so the Mini wins hands down for versatility. This leaves Fiat with their long tradition of tiny cars from the Topolino 500, to the 600 (1955–70) and Nuova 500 (1957–75) – cute like the Mini, but apart from independent suspension, not technically arousing. The rear-mounted engine and unsynchromeshed gearbox were unhelpful, but overall it was an incredibly successful small car. The performance Abarth versions were almost Cooperish.

It is hardly surprising that in May 1992 *Car Magazine* borrowed the oldest surviving Mini (621 AOK) from Rover and pitched it against the car that came closest in spirit to the old 500, and even shared its name, the Fiat Cinquecento. L.J.K. Setright refereed the bout. Of course, you cannot really compare cars separated by 33 years and

Setright did not try. The title of the feature was: 'Will there ever be a better mini than the Mini?' to which the answer has to be a resounding no. 'There is a new fashion for cars – to be as short as possible. The fact that none of them, not even the titchiest of the Japanese tax dodgers, is as short as the Mini makes me wonder where the progress has been made. The Mini was just 10ft long in 1959; even the Fiat 126 is longer than that, and the Cinquecento is longer still.' Setright soon discovered the flaws in the 'new' Cinquecento, not least that it had ambitions to be a conventional motor car. Worse still there was no spark of the originality or genius that distinguished the earlier 500 and 600. However, the conclusion was that, 'It is merely an extraordinarily convenient car that quickly becomes a surprisingly endearing one.'

A VISIT TO LONGBRIDGE

Rationally the Mini has been outclassed, outdated and overpriced for some time, but it remains unique. The incredible thing is not just that the Mini has managed to survive this long, but also the fact that it is built in the same place, in the same way, and in some cases by people who have spent their entire working lives on the Mini production line.

'Where are the robots?' is the obvious question from anyone familiar with automated car production. With a few crucial exceptions, making a Mini is virtually unchanged after nearly forty years of production. Although Issigonis designed the Mini so that it was easy to build, hence the prominent exterior seams, it is not an especially easy, or quick car to assemble. What the Mini requires is good, old-fashioned craft skills – it is better built in the 1990s than it has ever been thanks to improved techniques,

Not much has changed since 1959. The Minis look identical, the production methods are the same and even some of the workers on the line have been there all along.

technology and a team approach to working and solving problems on the line.

Pam Wearing, Corporate Communications Manager and employee since the BMC days does not need reminding that she has been around the factory almost as long as the little car. 'If you live in Longbridge and all your family worked at Austin, it is inevitable that you are going to join them, but I have never regretted coming here.' Not surprisingly as we enter the Old West Works where the body shells are put together, Pam meets and greets everyone on the line like old friends, because they are. Reg Phillips, Manufacturing Manager, steers me around this time warp, 'We've still got some of the original equipment from 1959, like the jigs for the windshield and fenders although the main

carousel went last Christmas.' What strikes you is the large number of real people involved at this stage of the process. Whereas the rest of the Rover plant is sparsely manned and robotized, the Mini is virtually hand built. The body pressings that make up the shell are hand welded, which means that pinpoint accuracy is impossible. So each body has to be fettled, tweaked and teased to perfection. This takes experience and Bill Banner with an astonishing forty years on the track works in the 'boneyard' putting the bodies right. 'I have seen almost no changes over the years, which is a good thing, because building a Mini is highly skilled and I really enjoy being on final rectification. There isn't a fault I can't cure and the quality of the car just gets better.'

There are not many women around, but Lyn Croft became the first gas welder in the mid 1980s and is now in charge of the Final Quality Audit. Using her eyes and gloved hands no body leaves the plant without her authorization. 'I love it here, the blokes are all such brilliant characters who like a laugh, but are respectful with it.'

Bearded Brian Dipple fits that description, having worked on the Mini line since January 1960. Like the others he has not seen too many changes over the years, 'Things are a lot more stable today, back in the '70s it was down tools every five minutes for one reason, or another.' Has he ever got a little bored? 'Never … but I enjoy the work and wouldn't want to work on any other car. In the early days we called the Mini the "Bubble", to keep the model secret we were told BMC were building a bubble car, so the name stuck: working on the bubble, bubble trouble.'

As Brian chuckles I reflect on the fact that he has probably had something to do with just about every Mini I have owned and he is a lot friendlier than a robot. 'I have shown dozens of Japanese visitors around here over the years and they always ask where the robots are and they sort of freak out when you tell them there aren't any.' Pam Wearing leads me out of the Old West Works and past the surreal sight of dozens of bare metal shells waiting for paint. So the next stop is Paint Shop 3, which is rather more high tech. Now the Mini takes its turn sandwiched between much more modern products like the MGF and Rover 100, which trundle along together on a monorail. The bodies are degreased, rustproofed, primed and painted. The Mini Coopers with their contrasting coloured roofs go through the painting process twice, once to be sprayed Almond Green and again after the body is 'bagged up' in brown paper enabling the roof to be painted white.

It is then a short walk to the final assembly track where Rover 100s and Minis mingle before all the vital organs are plumbed in. Suddenly it is much like any other car plant as trim and mechanicals are added to the constantly moving shells. There are no 'workers' at Rover, only 'associates'. The benefits of teamwork, a legacy from the company's link with Honda, are constantly stressed by Geoff Powell, the Principal Engineer in Mini Technical Support. But Geoff is not a dour salaryman, like everyone else he genuinely loves Minis. He has a classic Cooper at home, another which he is restoring, and he drives to work in an old MGB. 'It's got such a great character and really stands out from the crowd. We also never stop developing it on the line, everyone is encouraged to come up with ways of building it better. Compared to a 1959 Mini the only parts which are identical are the roof and windscreen surround.'

Minis are carefully lowered onto the engine and sub-frames then fitted in place by four associates – another 1959 throwback, as the opposite happens with most modern cars as these parts are bolted up into the shell. After that there are electrical diagnostic checks and the Mini is run on a rolling road before being parked in a holding area and trailered to your local dealer. It has taken around 50 hours to build a Mini, roughly double the time a modern supermini spends inside a factory.

Production is running at over 400 a week and more than half of that number go direct to Japan. They can be credited with keeping the car alive, although these Minis have a slightly different specification. A peek under the bonnet reveals an air conditioning unit shoehorned into an impossibly small space. Inside, there is a bracket for a distress flare, and what looks like a squash ball is pushed onto the edge of the bumper to avoid scraping sensitive shins.

1. Body Panels: Rover Group Body and Pressings in Swindon produce the majority of the panels, although the doors, dashboard and front valance are made by Camford Pressings of Llanelli.

2. Grille and Fenders: three jigs are used to spot weld the front end of the Mini together.

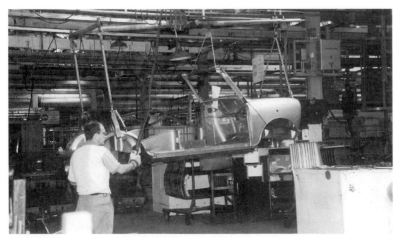

3. Floor: the floor pressings are joined to the front end and then put onto the build line.

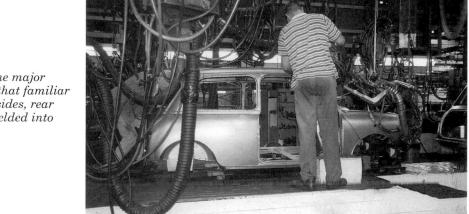

4. Monosides: all the major panels now box in that familiar Mini shape as the sides, rear end and roof are welded into place.

5. Doors, boot and bonnet: all the opening panels are screwed into place and the body trundles down an illuminated line to highlight any imperfections and where any rough areas are sanded off.

6. Final Line: off-line work is carried out for specific models and markets, such as cutting out the sunroof for a British Open, or detail changes for Japanese and other export specifications.

7. *VQ Final Quality Audit: every 'body in white' is checked for faults and will not leave the works until these are rectified and rechecked.*

8. *Dispatch: every body, still welded to its carrier, is moved to a holding area where it is stored until summoned by computer to the paint shop.*

9. *Paint shop: primer, underseal and final paint finish. A thoroughly modern approach to painting a very old body.*

10. Two-tone: a Cooper goes through the painting process twice on account of the contrasting roof colour.

11. Final Assembly Bodywork: glass, badging, stripes, lights, bumper and sundry other items are affixed.

12. Final Assembly Interior: dashboard, loom, air-conditioning, headlining and hundreds of other parts that conform to the Vehicle History Card. This identifies the model and specifies which parts need to be fitted.

13. Running Gear: as the shells are suspended in the air the A series engines built at the East works factory and the sub-frames, made by G.R. Smithson & Co of Wolverhampton, move along a lower track. The body is positioned over the running gear and exhaust system, then fixed in place on the moving line.

14. Checks: once the wheels have been bolted on, the Minis are treated to a full diagnostic test – rolling road, emissions, wipers, horn, lights, instrument accuracy and brake performance (not illustrated).

15. Completion: finished Minis are parked outside the factory in the summer sunshine awaiting the transporter that will take them to your local dealer.

6 All That Glitters – The Special Editions

'Mini Cock-Ups, the lot of them.'

Rowan Atkinson

Just when the Mini looked as though it was heading for retirement in the 1980s, Austin Rover suddenly discovered that they could never create enough special editions. In marketing terms these were a relatively simple repackaging exercise, which meant that it brought the car to the public's attention for a token outlay. For the price of some decals, maybe a snazzy paint scheme and a creative approach to the options list, the Mini was dangled in front of consumers who behaved as if the car had never existed. The truth was that many buyers needed reminding that the Mini was still on sale and this was a cheap way of doing it; certainly a lot cheaper than spending serious development money to upgrade the car mechanically.

It was not just in the UK that the specials struck a chord. In certain markets, like Japan and France, they could not get enough of them. The Mini may have been a mass market 'people's car' but it was now the most

Under all those 'period' extras is the first in a long line of limited edition Minis.

niche of niche automotive products. As every limited edition sold out, the accounts department celebrated as profits and volumes soared. The special edition syndrome was not a new phenomenon; BMC had begun celebrating production milestones with the millionth Minors, badged 'Minor 1,000,000'. The Mini first entered the special edition zone in 1976 and this trend looks set to continue for as long as the car stays in production.

One can only speculate what Issigonis made of such frivolous marketing exercises, but to the Mini purist each adventure down the slippery special edition route was a disaster. Writing in 1991 about a Mini Cooper that *Car Magazine* were giving away in a competition, Rowan Atkinson took the time to identify the enduring appeal of the Mini and launch a well deserved attack on the roll call of minimum production Minis. 'Endless limited editions have attempted to maintain the appeal with only cosmetic titivation. We hereby recall, with fond memories, the Mini Sprite, Ritz, Chelsea, Designer, Advantage, Park Lane, 30, Studio 2, Sky, Flame, Rose, 25, Checkmate, Piccadilly, Jet Black, Red Hot, Flaming Stupid. An absurd Odyssey of marketingspeak, being merely applications of make-up to what was perceived to be a tired old face, when in fact the Mini has elegant, classical features, that are ruined by crude face paint. Mini Cock-Ups, the lot of them.'

Just in case you wondered about the name, launch date, approximate production and retail price of all those Minis, here in full are 20 years of special editions. Production figures are for the UK only.

LIMITED EDITION (3,000) – JANUARY 1976

This is where it all started. With no particular anniversary in mind – not that any manufacturer ever needs an excuse – British Leyland introduced the cosmetically enhanced Mini Limited Edition at £1,406. Based on the 1000, the paintwork was green and white with a gold coachline. If that was not bad enough a distinctly 1970s interior had orange-striped brush nylon seats similar in style to contemporary MGB upholstery. At least the seats reclined and there were eyeball fresh air vents, yet to become standard on the 1000. This was the style of things to come although the British public had to wait three years for another special edition.

1100 SPECIAL (5,100) – AUGUST 1979

This was the first and one of the very few Mini limited editions with a point: the celebration of twenty years of Mini production at £3,300. It was the most clearly thought out special edition, with tangible differences from the standard model. Consequently it was also the most successful, as the projected run of 2,500 was upped to 5,000 units, with 5,100 eventually shifted.

Based on the 1000, with the familiar Mark III body, there the similarity ended. Under the bonnet was the Clubman's 1,098cc, 45bhp engine. This meant better than 998cc average performance with an 84mph (135kph) top speed and sprightly 16.6 seconds for 0–60mph acceleration. On the outside, customers could choose Rose metallic paint with tan vinyl roof, or Silver metallic with black vinyl on top. Graded side stripes ran a little above the sills, leading to prominent matt black wheel arch extensions, over wide 165/70 tyres that surrounded 5 × 10 alloys. On the front wings were side indicators. There were Clubman bumpers front and rear, a locking petrol cap, tinted glass and a 'Special' badge on the boot lid.

On the inside the Special had numerous 1275GT features, including a sports steering wheel, centre console and three-instrument binnacle. A radio, clock, lighter and cubby tray occupied the console and there was even more storage space with an additional tray above the passenger's knee. Tartan check upholstery and cut pile carpets completed the highly successful picture.

SPRITE (2,500) – OCTOBER 1983

Based on the City, the Sprite had bright Primula Yellow or Cinnabar Red paint with wide side stripes separated by a 'Sprite' logo on the rear side panels. There were several carry-overs from the 1100 Special, including identical alloys and wheel arch extensions. Inside were a three-dial binnacle, eyeball vents and a four-spoke steering wheel. The seats had grey herringbone material topped off with black plastic head restraints. The price was £3,334.

25 (5,000) – JULY 1984

Another celebration required another Mini special, this time for the car's 25th birthday. The silver anniversary meant giving a Mayfair a silver paint job, a bucket load of logos and a price tag of £3,865. A grey and red coachline ran around the bodywork with Mini 25 on the rear panels, boot and even the wheel centres. A silver-grey paint scheme extended to the wheel arches, bumpers, grille, door mirrors and handles.

The silver '25' theme extended to the interior with 25 logoed Flint velvet seat trim (the front seats even had zippered pockets in front of the squabs), edged with red piping plus grey and red carpets. A three-instrument binnacle faced the driver, who grabbed hold of a leather bound steering wheel with '25' on the boss. Entertainment

came in the shape of a radio cassette conveniently positioned for passenger operation, with two rear parcel shelf mounted speakers ready to fill the cabin with noise. The most notable innovation was the 12in wheels and front discs, which had yet to find their way onto the standard production car.

RITZ (3,725) – JANUARY 1985

The first of the mid-1980s special edition cascade involved tarting up a basic City. The initial theme was upmarket London locations, hence the Ritz at £3,798. Obviously Austin Rover were inspired by the success of the 25 as this model had a silver leaf metallic paint scheme. A red triple coachline ran around the body, broken up with Ritz logos on the rear side panels and boot lid.

Nimbus Grey paint was used to colour key the grille, wheel arches, roof gutter and driver's door mirror. There was more grey on the alloy wheels and proper chrome on the door handles, bumpers, boot handle and even the exhaust pipe. Inside the Mayfair-equipped cockpit there were more Ritz logos on the seats with colourful red, blue and grey velvet striped trim. Blue extended to the fascia, seat belts, carpets and door pockets.

CHELSEA (1,500) – JANUARY 1986

The SW postcode theme continued with the Chelsea at £3,898. It was based on the City E and followed a familiar pattern, with Mayfair instrumentation, alloy wheels and three Chelsea logos on the outside and on the seats. Although the seat trim was grey with red piping the exterior colour was Targa Red with twin red and silver coachlines.

The Mini Chelsea.

PICCADILLY (2,500) – MAY 1986

Austin Rover had hit their stride by now and moved into the West End with the Piccadilly: yet another City E, this time with full width plastic wheel trims, although chrome made a welcome return to the bumpers and door handles. Cashmere Gold was the exterior colour, while the velvet interior was dark and beverage-based: Chocolate, Coffee and Claret. It was priced at £3,928.

This model set the trend for most future limited editions, having few luxurious

Mini Piccadilly.

touches but plenty of cosmetic frippery. The standard push-button radio, head restraints and three-spoke steering wheel were not much to get excited about, yet these packages proved to be a roaring success in the home and export markets.

PARK LANE (4,000) – JANUARY 1987

The final model in the otherwise curious quartet of London based limited editions saw Rover back in Mayfair with the Park Lane at £4,194. Its all-black paintwork was contrasted by chrome bumpers and door handles. The logo was a little more bold, occupying the lower part of the rear panel and extending onto the door. Inside was stripy beige and black velvet, plus logos and a stereo radio cassette.

ADVANTAGE (4,675) – MAY 1987

This previously untapped seasonal theme proved popular enough for the company to return to it repeatedly over the years. If the Queen's Club had obliged, this could have been the Mini Wimbledon; instead it remained the Advantage, launched to coincide with Wimbledon Fortnight.

Of course, the colour scheme had to be pure Diamond White, with colour keyed wheel trims. The logo featured a tiny tennis ball full stop and running along the flanks was a pattern inspired by a tennis net. Otherwise it was City E, with matt black bumpers, grille, wheel arches and door handle. Inside, there was the usual Mayfair instrument installation with more tennis net upholstery patterns finished in grey and green. It would set you back £4,286.

Mini Park Lane.

JET BLACK, RED HOT (6,000) – JANUARY 1988

Red Hot (left) and Jet Black (right).

As the names suggested, the Red Hot was painted red with contrasting black coachline and logo. The Jet Black was exactly the opposite. What they both had in common were chrome bumpers and door handles with silver and red lined wheel trims. Inside were black velour seats with red piping, black carpets and trim. On the grille was an identifying badge. Tinted glass, a push-button radio and a three-spoke steering wheel were all part of the very simple package. Both types cost £4,382.

DESIGNER (2,000) – JUNE 1988

The Designer Mini is the point at which Rover fully embraced 1980s marketing values without a hint of irony. There was a proposal to name it the Mini Mary Quant to associate the special edition with the Swinging

Mini Designer.

Sixties. In the end they settled on Designer at £4,654 – although the Mary Quant daisy logo survived on the bonnet in place of the usual Mini badge and her influence extended to a heavily branded Quant interior.

The car was available in either black or white; the usual items of chrome or matt black exterior trim were finished in grey. Inside, the upholstery was black and white striped with Quant's signature on each seat. The leather trimmed steering wheel had another Quant daisy on the boss and the driver even had a vanity mirror to gaze into.

RACING, FLAME (2,000) – JANUARY 1989

Here Rover were feeling their way back towards the retro appeal of the Cooper. The

Racing at £4,795 was finished in British Racing Green with a contrasting white roof while the Flame was red and white. Unfortunately alloy wheels were not on the Cooperesque menu, owners had to make do with full width white trims, but a couple of nods in the direction of performance were the sports steering wheel and rev counter.

ROSE, SKY (1,000) – JANUARY 1989

The Rose and Sky were Rover's soft touch to the hard-nosed Racing and Flame. The colour schemes for these models were almost offensive, finished in white with either a pastel blue (Sky) or pastel pink (Rose) roof. It got even worse inside, with pink and blue upholstery! The price was £4,695.

1989 Special Editions; (from top left) Rose, Sky, Flame and Racing.

THIRTY (3,000) – JUNE 1989

This edition, based on the Mayfair, wished the Mini a happy 30th birthday. Not only was it rather good in terms of presentation and equipment, it also represented a watershed in modern Mini development, providing the basis for the re-launch of the Cooper.

The effort put into the two pearlescent paint colours – red and black – was the most immediately striking feature, and was given extra sheen by a coat of lacquer. The logo was more of a crest, with elements of the old Austin marque crossed with rampant British lions and the legend '1959–1989' running beneath it. A feature of the bonnet badge, the crest was also applied to the rear side panels with twin coachlines leading from them.

The door mirrors and wheel arches were colour matched, but the most welcome retro element was the increase in brightwork, as the grille, door handles and bumpers shone brightly again. Best of all, the car sat on eight-spoke Minilite-type alloys. As usual the interior had seat logos, but there was a real touch of luxury about the black leather

Mini Thirty.

(Below)
1990 Special Editions; (from left) Flame Red, Check Mate and Racing Green.

seat bolster, red piping, red leather steering wheel with a logo on the boss and red pile carpet. Not only that, there was a leather-bound Mini book waiting for every buyer who could find the £5,599 asking price.

RACING GREEN, FLAME RED, CHECK MATE (2,500) – FEBRUARY 1990

These models were the clearest indications yet that a full scale Cooper revival was just around the corner. Two old names were lengthened into Racing Green and Flame Red and were joined by a new one, Check Mate. They all sold for £5,455 and had chrome bumpers, those lovely eight-spoke alloys and two-tone paint schemes, the Check Mate being black with a white roof. They all had a crossed chequered flag badge on the bonnet and inside was black seat trim and a three-instrument binnacle.

A significant technical uprate was the adoption of the original Cooper S final drive ratio of 3.44:1. An automatic gearbox was an option – but the most existing

add-on goody was the Rover-approved John Cooper performance kit, which really turned it into a Cooper.

STUDIO 2 (2,000) – JUNE 1990

Just when we thought that Rover were getting the hang of these special editions they went back to their bad old ways – maybe they had some old graphics left over from a Metro Special of the same name last seen in 1987 and 1988. The logos were stuck to the front edge of the doors and the rest was predictable and based on a City: the grille was now chrome, but the bumpers were not. Colour schemes were black, blue, or grey. Inside, there were doeskin seat covers with a green diagonal stripe. The Studio 2 cost £5,455.

1990 MINI-MINOR

Here is a special edition that never was. Occasionally Rover's Special Vehicles Department came up with a concept that did not hit the marketing spot; although rejected, this one

Mini-Minor.

sneaked out. Based on the Studio 2, it was intended specifically for the Japanese market as a 30th anniversary special edition.

The idea was to make a modern copy of the oldest production Mini, registered 621 AOK and parked in the Heritage Motor Centre. It was painted a very special creamy shade of Old English White, and apparently the Special Vehicles Department went so far as to stick on dummy exterior door hinges and Mark I hub caps. The original red and cream upholstery was copied, but stripped out before the car was sold. However, the red carpets, headlining and unique 'M' logo gear knob remained.

NEON (1,500) – FEBRUARY 1991

Yet another City with an unwise makeover at £5,835. The name suggested brightness, when it was in fact quite dull. The only real bright spots were the chromework – on bumpers, door handles, the grille and the exhaust pipe. Nordic Blue metallic was the prevailing colour scheme, offset by a coachline leading back to a slightly bizarre 'Neon by Mini' logo. Mayfair wheel trims and a passenger door mirror did not whip up too much excitement, and the Chevron velour upholstery hardly grabbed the attention.

BRITISH OPEN CLASSIC (1,000) – JUNE 1992

Rover were after some golfing allusion plus a dodgy pun with this one, but the results were impressive. This was the first limited edition based on the 1.3 Mini and also the first time a British model had an opening sunroof. And what a sunroof: an electrically operated, full length fabric affair.

The coat of arms made an impressive comeback on the rear panels and bonnet badge and Rover also stitched a 'By appointment to Her Majesty the Queen' label into the front seats! Those lovely alloys were back and so was all the other chrome, although the door mirrors were colour-keyed metallic British Racing Green. A wind deflector kept out draughts from above and inside there was true luxury: Countryman Tweed upholstery with leather seats and steering wheel. It was well worth the £7,195.

Mini Neon.

Mini British Open Classic.

(Below*)*
Italian Job Special Editions.

ITALIAN JOB (1,750) – OCTOBER 1992

A special edition waiting to happen since the 1969 film, the Italian Job turned out to be a big disappointment. Despite a jaunty crossed British and Italian flag logo on the bonnet and rear panels, this model failed to excite. One reason was the standard 1,275cc engine under the bonnet, a long way off Cooper tune.

The appearance was meant to resemble the cars featured in the film; although red, white or blue versions were offered, most cars were finished in British Racing Green, a colour never used on the screen cars. Bonnet stripes echoed the Cooper, rather than the bonnet strapped film stars' Minis, and there were just two spot lamps, rather than three. The alloys were curiously painted white as was the grille, which resembled a Mark I Minor. Inside was black tweed trim and the Mayfair's instruments. Clearly Rover were building this model to a price so they could sell it for £5,995 – if anyone really wanted a car like those in the film they simply bought a Cooper.

RIO (750) – JUNE 1993

Another mid-1990s example of Rover getting lazy, this spruced-up Mini Sprite at £5,495 amounted to no more than special paintwork. It came with pearlescent Caribbean Blue, Black or metallic Polynesian Turquoise, with Rio logos and black interior. The internal bonnet release and radio cassette were at least useful.

TAHITI (500) – OCTOBER 1993

If there is any significance to be gained by looking at the production figures, 500 units might reflect the lessening popularity of the standard Mini as buyers flocked to the Cooper. The nicest things about the Tahiti were the alloys and perhaps the Tahiti Blue paintwork. The chrome bumpers were smart, but Rover penny-pinched by not fitting opening

Mini Rio.

(Below*)*
Mini Tahiti.

rear windows. The interior was only notable for having new style seats, while the trim was predominantly finished in black. The Tahiti cost £5,795 – if anyone was interested, an automatic version was almost £1,000 extra.

35 (200) – JUNE 1994

With the 35, Rover missed a prime opportunity. Whereas previous anniversary cars had at least made an effort to stand out from the mainstream Mini crowd, the 35 was understated to the point of anonymity. It was based on the Sprite and the colour options were white, pearlescent red and a metallic blue with a silver side stripe. Chrome was on the menu, dished out in the direction of bumpers, grille and door handles. Unique '35' logos on the rear flanks and bonnet badge were the only clues that this model was something special. Things perked up inside with so called Jamboree trim, a blue and pink concoction that partly covered the seats and doors, but that was it. Hardly good value at £6,695.

1994 Mini 35 SE with 1959 Mini.

Mini Sidewalk.

(Below)
This is what the special edition syndrome had come to by 1996 – the triumph of 'style' over substance. This was the confusing image used in press advertising for the EquinoX SE to suggest that the Mini was a fashion statement.

SIDEWALK (1,000) – MAY 1995

The £5,895 Sidewalk was the standard Sprite makeover. Once again there were three colour options: White Diamond, Charcoal metallic and Kingfisher Blue. The latest in a long line of slightly bizarre logos included an obvious Side Walk reference, while a star design stamp oddly proclaimed 'Authentic Mini'. Inside, it was authentically Caledonian as vivid blue tartan trim contrasted with the red seat belts.

EQUINOX – APRIL 1996

Described as the 'Heavenly Mini EquinoX' this special edition was designed for some reason around a Zodiac theme. The decals comprised a large sun surrounded by the moon and stars, all very new age and £6,195. As ever, there were three colours: Pearlescent Amaranth Purple, Charcoal metallic and Platinum Silver metallic. Chrome bumpers and grille were standard along with tinted glass and opening rear quarterlights. The Sun, Moon and Stars theme was woven in purple into the upholstery.

7 Variations on a Mini Theme: Vans, Estates, Elfs, Hornets and Mokes

'Curiously prophetic of the 1963 Ferrari LM.'

Laurence Pomeroy on the Mini Pick Up

If any production car lent itself to being adapted, developed and derived, it had to be the Mini. With the drivetrain neatly packaged at the front in its own sub-frame it could be stretched, adorned and stripped, hence the variations that took the Mini concept to its limits. It did not take long for there to be a Mini for every job and every eventuality.

VAN – BUSINESS TOOL

This model was a pretty crucial element in the success of the Mini. Previous big hits in the light commercial vehicle (LCV) market were 210,000 Austin A30/35 vans and more than 325,000 Morris Minor vans and pick ups. That was profitable business, so Leonard Lord wasted no time introducing a Mini LCV.

Morris Mini Van in action.

A mere five months after the launch of the saloon, BMC revealed its first commercial derivative in January 1960. Based on the saloon floor pan, the van wheelbase was stretched by 4in (102mm). Up to the B pillars it was standard Mini, beyond that it was pure panel van. A raised load platform in the floor added the necessary structural rigidity, and the spare wheel and battery were housed in a gap immediately behind the front seats. Right at the back, adjacent to the axle, was a specially designed oblong fuel tank that held 6 gallons (27 litres). The rear suspension was modified with longer turrets, which stiffened and raised the ride and lifted the rear end. What all this added up to was a usefully low loading height of just over 17in (432mm) and 46cu ft (1,303 litres) of load space. Turf out the passenger and remove their seat (an optional extra anyway) and this space increased to 58cu ft (1,643 litres). There was a lengthy 55in (1,397mm) of space from doors to seats and almost 54in (1,372mm) of width to play with, so it could accommodate some surprisingly large objects. The payload was officially 5cwt (250kg), but users soon exceeded that weight on a regular basis.

Laurence Pomeroy was quick to point out in his book *The Mini Story* how much better was the ADO 15 LCV when compared to the 1956 A35 version, the principal reason being the front-wheel-drive layout. He pointed out that 'The earlier design had an overall length of 11 feet 6 inches and was thus 8 inches longer than the Mini van, but the platform length was 53 inches, 2 inches shorter. The distance from the floor to the roof was the same on both vehicles, although the more recently designed [Mini] was only 52 inches high as compared with 64 inches on the earlier [A35]. It is in addition 225 pounds lighter and had a platform 8 inches nearer the ground.'

The specification was kept to the bare minimum. At the front, the grille was simply stamped out of the front panel (the approach Issigonis had originally envisaged for the no-frills Minor and Seven), restricting maintenance access. At the back there were quarter bumpers, which at least did not get in the way when loading. Inside was the minimum of trim with lots of metalwork on show and a heavy-duty floor covering. Even a rear view mirror was an option as the wing mirrors satisfied the minimum legal requirement.

ALL MOD CONS

Despite the spartan specification, the Mini Van proved to be very popular with private customers, not least because the price was £360 as opposed to the saloon's £497. The difference was Purchase Tax, which was not payable on commercial vehicles. All the owners had to do was refrain from cutting out windows in the side panels and keep their top speed to 30mph (48kph) – except on the new M1 motorway where they could speed up to 40mph (64kph) – and the van qualified as commercial and for tax purposes as a business tool. In fact, Mini Vans proved to be very popular with Mods in the early 1960s. They regarded the car as modern and smart with a useful amount of rear space for a dead Lambretta, or just to crash out in after a hectic weekend in Brighton. A Mini Van was certainly a lot less draughty and more reliable than a scooter.

Not surprisingly, for owners who wanted to carry two extra passengers in some degree of comfort, after-market conversion kits quickly became available. BMC marketed their own kit, which retailed at just

How to boost the passenger-swallowing abilities of your van in three easy stages by using a BMC conversion kit (opposite).

HOW TO CONVERT YOUR MINI-VAN INTO A 4-SEATER

WITHOUT REDUCING ITS CARRYING CAPACITY

There's a Mini-Van Conversion Kit for both Austin and Morris models. It provides comfortable seating for two more passengers. Yet, fold the seats away, and you have exactly the same payload capacity as before the conversion. You can do the conversion yourself — all you need is a reasonable set of tools — or you can have your garageman fit it for you.

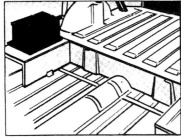

Section of false floor cut away to take seat.

Conversion completed, your 4-seater saloon awaits.

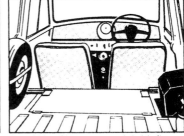

Seats fold swiftly away, van ready to take its usual big load.

MINI-VAN CONVERSION KIT

for **AUSTIN** and **MORRIS** models Price complete £14.5.0. PVC-bound carpet—£3.7.3 extra (Inc. P.T.)
Complete kit—all you need plus detailed instructions—is available now from your Austin or Morris Distributor or Dealer. Only they supply the kits carrying B.M.C.'s 12-month warranty

B·M·C SERVICE LIMITED COWLEY · OXFORD

over £15 and used parts from the estate car. A contemporary advertisement showed how easy it was for the DIY motorist to install. A section of the false floor was cut away and the seat filled the gap between the rear wheel arches. The only problem was that rear passengers rubbed shoulders with the relocated battery and spare wheel. Nevertheless, with the rear seats folded flat the load bay was just as big and flat as before unlike many modern hatchbacks with split fold seating arrangements. PVC-bound carpets were an optional extra.

Of course, the best customers were those who were going to put them to work and the country's biggest LCV fleets took the little vans to their hearts. They proved to be very useful for the Post Office and the Police, while AA patrolmen breathed a sigh of relief at getting a proper, weatherproof car instead of an uncomfortable motorcycle and sidecar combination.

VAN TURNS 95

At the launch in 1960 there were two models, the Austin Se7en Van and the Morris Minivan, distinguished only by their badging. To some extent these models existed in their own time warp, almost untouched by saloon developments. In 1962, when the clumsy Se7en designation was dropped to become simply the Austin Mini Van, such luxuries as windscreen washers, an interior light and bumper overriders became standard. By 1967 the 998cc engine became an option; with 3.44:1 final drive although it was not especially popular.

In 1969 a range name change turned all the models simply into Mini Vans. This coincided with the adoption of negative Earth electrics and a mechanical fuel pump. In the 1970s the synchromesh was improved, a rod-operated gear change was introduced, and the interior

was uprated with rocker switches and column stalks. In late 1978 'Mini 95' badges showed the designated gross weight of the van. A year later a touch of luxury courtesy of the 'L' pack brought cloth-faced seats, carpets, a passenger sun visor and extra sound deadening as standard to the 1000 and optional on the 850. In 1983 the Mini Van was replaced by the roomier but unlovable Metro Van.

PICK UP – MINI TOOL 2

The next logical commercial development after the Mini Van had to be the Mini Pick Up, which arrived a year later in 1961. It was largely identical to the van except for the missing roof and side panels. Adding strength to the structure was a bulkhead directly behind the front seats with a flat rear window. The flat deck led to a tailgate that was secured by two hinged arms and, like the saloon, there was a hinged number plate, which allowed full-length loads to be carried completely legally. It also had van-like versatility because an optional (later standard) canvas cover could be erected over two steel hoops and tailed off with a transparent plastic rear screen.

Development mirrored updates to the van. The 850 version was the first to be discontinued in 1980. The 1000 model lived as long as the Van but in May 1983 it left the price lists, never to be replaced. The commercials inhabited a stubbornly Mark 1 body that never grew up. Neither flirted with Hydrolastic suspension or faddish, Clubman style updates. External door hinges, door levers, sliding windows, door bins and shoe print rear lights survived on the commercials until they were discontinued in the 1980s. They were a fabulous throwback to a simpler automotive era and perhaps the models that remained closest to the Issigonis ideal.

Van (January 1960 to May 1983); Pick Up (February 1961 to October 1980)

Engine

Type	Four cylinder in line; cast iron block transversely mounted in front
Capacity	848cc (1,000cc from 1969)
Bore and stroke	62.94mm × 68.26mm
Output	34bhp at 5,500rpm
Compression ratio	8.3:1
Maximum torque	44lb.ft at 2,900rpm

Transmission

Type	Front-wheel drive
Gear ratios	4-speed 3.765/5.317/8.176/13.657 13.657 (reverse) (final drive)

Suspension

Front	Wishbones, rubber cones, Armstrong dampers
Rear	Trailing arms, rubber cones, Armstrong dampers
Steering	Rack and pinion

Brakes   Hydraulic drum/drum

Tyres/Wheels   5.2in × 10in cross-ply/3.5in × 10in

Dimensions

Track (front)	47.375in (1,203mm)
Track (rear)	45.875in (1,165mm)
Wheelbase	84.16in (2,138mm)
Length	Van 129.9in (3,299mm)
	Pick Up 130.5in (3,315mm); 130.2in (3,307mm) from 1970
Width	55in (1,397mm)
Height	Van 53.5in (1,359mm)
	Pick Up 53.3in (1,354mm)
Unladen weight	Van 1,334lb (605kg); 1,371lb (622kg) from 1969
	Pick Up 1,328lb (602kg); 1,369lb (621kg) from 1969
Load	Van 46cu ft (1,302 litres); 58cu ft (1,642 litres) with passenger seat removed
	Pick Up 26.75cu ft (758 litres) with rear tonneau cover on
Fuel capacity	6 gallons (27 litres)

Performance

Top speed	850 72mph (116kph)
	1000 75mph (121kph)
Acceleration	850 0–60mph in 34 seconds
	1000 0–60mph in 22 seconds
Fuel consumption	40mpg (7 litres per 100km)

Purchase price   £360

Production

Van	521,494
Pick Up	58,179

MINI ESTATES

Having successfully extended the Mini floor pan to accommodate Van bodywork it was only a matter of time before windows were installed to mark the arrival of the estate versions. The Austin Se7en Countryman and Morris Mini-Traveller were launched in September 1960. These new vehicles were obviously based on the wheelbase of the van, but there the similarity ended. The estates weighed around 110lb (50kg) more than the van as a result of the fixtures and fittings. The luxurious touches included a trimmed fuel tank, headlining, carpets and hardly a bare piece of metal on show.

Outside, the most notable difference was the extensive exterior woodwork, which the marketing department had deemed necessary to cultivate an upmarket gentrified image. This was an indulgence that Issigonis was violently opposed to, but he was not successful in getting it removed. This mock Tudor beam work did however connect the models with other BMC estates, principally the Morris Minor Traveller. That estate needed the wood to hold the rear of the car together, whereas on the Mini Countryman and Traveller it was entirely non-structural. The timber was simply glued onto the rear side panels behind the B panel and on the twin rear doors. Also adding to the weight were rear seats and the De Luxe level of trim, although like the van, a rear view mirror was on the options list. The rear windows were positively panoramic and also offered plenty of welcome ventilation because like the ones at the front, they were sliding affairs.

Compared to the paltry 5.5cu ft (156 litres) of boot space of the saloon, the estates offered cavernous accommodation. With the

A 'woody' Mini Estate somewhere in the Home Counties.

**Austin Countryman/Morris Traveller (September 1960 to October 1967);
Austin Countryman/Morris Traveller 1000 Mark II (October 1967 to October 1969)**

Engine
Type	Four cylinder in line; cast iron block transversely mounted in front
Capacity	848cc/998cc
Bore and stroke	62.94mm × 68.26mm/64.6mm × 76.2mm
Output	34bhp at 5,500rpm/38bhp at 5,250rpm
Compression ratio	8.3:1
Maximum torque	44lb.ft at 2,900rpm/52lb.ft at 2,700rpm

Transmission
Type	Front-wheel drive
Gear ratios	4-speed 3.765/5.317/8.176/13.657 13.657 (reverse) (final drive)

Suspension
Front	Wishbones, rubber cones, Armstrong dampers
Rear	Trailing arms, rubber cones, Armstrong dampers
Steering	Rack and pinion

Brakes Hydraulic drum/drum

Tyres/Wheels 5.2in × 10in cross-ply/3.5in × 10in

Dimensions
Track (front)	47.375in (1,203mm)
Track (rear)	45.875in (1,165mm)
Wheelbase	84.25in (2,140mm)
Length	129.9in (3,299mm)
Width	55in (1,397mm)
Height	53.5in (1,359mm)
Unladen weight	1,484lb (673kg)/1,455lb (660kg)
Luggage capacity	18.5cu ft (524 litres); 35.3cu ft (1,000 litres) with seats folded
Fuel capacity	6.5 gallons (29 litres)

Performance
Top speed	69mph (111kph)/72mph (116kph)
Acceleration	0–60mph in 33/27 seconds
Fuel consumption	38mpg (7.4 litres per 100km)/34mpg (8.3 litres per 100km)

Purchase price £623/£629

Production 197,600
Mark I	161,000
Mark 2	46,000

rear seats folded it was 35.3cu ft (1,000 litres), and even with four occupants there was 18.5cu ft (524 litres). To cope with the load it had stiffer van suspension and the weight distribution was biased more to the rear than in the saloon. At the back there was no room for the spare wheel and battery so they were positioned under the floor where the van's petrol tank had been. That meant that the estates used the saloon's tank, positioned bulkily at the rear nearside of the load area. Power was provided by the standard 848cc unit so these vehicles struggled to 70mph (113kph), were slightly slower off the mark than the saloon and were thirstier by around 2mpg (0.5l/100km). But they more than made up for these deficiencies with considerable practicality.

ESTATES ON TEST

Autocar seemed to like the package when they tested an Estate in September 1960. 'Already holding a reputation of being a great little car, this latest version will certainly enhance this assessment. For town use it remains easy to park, and is fast through traffic because of its compact dimensions. On the open road its performance is adequate to transport four people and luggage with considerable economy and ease.'

Motor tested an untimbered Mini Countryman for 1,734 miles (2,791km). The magazine pronounced, 'Having long put up with the difficulty of wedging articles on the back seat, the shopping housewife will find the low loading ease of the Countryman a big attraction, for the Mini is the lowest of all; dog and carry-cot are both so much more easily catered for. Just as comfortable and acceptable as the Jones's four door saloon, estate cars no longer carry the stigma of a "trade" vehicle.' They also undertook a slightly bizarre test to see how many lions

they could pack into the back of their Countryman – 1,764 in the form of eggs stamped with the distinctive lion logo of the Egg Marketing Board. That translated into four large boxes of eggs, plus eighteen further packs containing six eggs each. There was room for many more if rearward vision was not to be a priority.

In their performance tables, *Motor* compared the Mini statistically with its rivals, long before the comparative road test became commonplace. The Mini lost out slightly to the Austin A40 on maximum speed, but was by far the most impressive in acceleration terms. The otherwise unremarkable Fiat Giardiniera beat the Mini's fuel consumption. Overall, the A40, Fiat, Ford Anglia Estate and Hillman Husky were also-rans compared to the thoroughly modern Mini.

Consistent Mini fan John Bolster, writing in *Autosport*, made a convincing case for the mock-Tudor timber. 'The shooting brake, station wagon, utility, call it what you will, is an extremely popular type of dual purpose vehicle. When I was a boy, a certain aura surrounded these machines, and I don't mean just the scent of varnished timber of which they were constructed. Chauffeur driven, they whispered down the long gravel drives of the big houses, taking beaters to the shoot or collecting guests from the train. One kept the chassis of last year's Rolls and sent it to the coachbuilders for such a conversion, after which it became the most useful form of transport that any family could possess. There has been a revolution and the spacious days are no more.'

Even so, the Mini did not disappoint. 'The Traveller which I took over was resplendent in white paint and varnished wood and I had to admit that it was monstrously handsome. I purposely drove to fetch it in my own Mini, so that a comparison would be immediate, and I at once admired the better quality of the carpets, upholstery and interior trim. I found that the little brake had a slightly better gear change with rather more effective synchromesh.'

METAL AND MARK II

For these models, 1962 proved to be an interesting year. The clumsy Se7en name was dropped – to everyone's relief – and BMC marketed an all-steel version of the Estate. First produced for export purposes a year earlier, this unadorned model represented a saving of £19 and quite a few planks of wood. In all other respects the models were identical, with De Luxe specifications. Development thereafter followed the saloon. Like the van there was no experimentation with Hydrolastic suspension and an automatic gearbox was never an option.

When the Mark II Countryman and Traveller were introduced in October 1967 the big news was the adoption of the 998cc engine. At last the little Estate could lug heavier loads without getting left behind. Apart from the facelifted front end, the model remained largely as before. Both woody and plain metal versions were on sale, the price differential remaining £19. There were rear sliding windows as before and the footprint rear light clusters were not replaced by the saloon's shoe boxes.

CUBIC CLUBMAN

At a stroke, British Leyland rationalized their range of small estate cars. They also horrified traditionalists by repackaging these models in Clubman clothing. Out went the cuddly old woodies and in came the

Mini Clubman Estate pictured in 1973, complete with unmissable vinyl coated, wood effect, steel battens on the flanks and rear doors.

The load carrying is still advertised but perhaps a shade less optimistically than in 1959.

cubed Clubman with vinyl coated steel side trims: it looked like a particularly narrow Formica sideboard. At least the square front looked more at home on the longer Estate bodywork, even if the fake wood trims that ran down the flanks and around to the rear doors took a bit of getting used to.

Generally the press welcomed the new range. *Autocar* went and bought one to run for an extended test and were a little disappointed when they reported to their readers after 10,000 miles (16,000km). Build quality on collection was hardly inspiring: with just 22 miles (34km) on the clock there was no handbook, both rear ashtrays were missing, the rear number plate lamp glass was cracked, and all the carpets were unclipped and badly fitted. Mechanically, things were not much better as there were noisy tappets, an exhaust popping on the over-run, squeaky pedals and heavy fuel consumption. Not only that, the speedometer, universal joints and carburettor needles were replaced during the test period.

Developments over the years were as the saloon Clubman. A single door mirror replaced the wing variety in 1973. Most significantly, in 1975, the 1,098cc engine became the standard manual gearbox power unit, while 998cc models were automatic only. In 1977 BL admitted that the mock wood was pretty risible and replaced it with cheaper side stripes. Significantly, the Clubman Estate was not killed off immediately by the arrival of the all-new Metro – there were surplus stocks to be sold. Technically it could be called a hatchback, and certainly it was no bigger than the more modern superminis, but by comparison it was hopelessly outclassed.

CLUBMAN VERSUS HOLDALLS

In June 1973 *Motor* cottoned on to the emerging trend for so-called superminis, although they called them 'budget holdalls'. 'The starting point ... was the Renault 5, a car which embodies no technical innovation – indeed it was built up largely from existing components – but which does, we believe, represent a landmark in packaging and styling with its roomy and versatile three door body ... It brings to the small car class the rear door and the estate form of bodywork which we

The legendary A series engine. This is an immaculate 998cc Cooper unit.

Old Minis never die, or at least they don't have to. CKR 584T was a tired and rusty yellow Mini 1000 before Oxford Mini Specialists rebuilt it with a low mileage engine, new panels, subframe, clutch and brakes for owner Carol Goulden.

Bank Garage custom built this pick up with over £1,000 worth of joinery gracing the load bay.

Distinctive, blunt Mini Clubman front end which may have dated, but thankfully offered mechanics more knuckle room.

A real one off. This concours winning Rover Mini Minor belonging to Lynn Thompson with unique badging and trim was an attempt to interest the Japanese market in a retro look Mini which sadly never got beyond the prototype stage. Finished in Old English White, it originally had an early '60s Austin Red interior. It had the designation ADO 20/3D/90.

A racing Mini Se7en in the paddock at Snetterton, Norfolk, in summer 1996.

A very rare 1961 Mini Super in 'original' condition pictured in Bank garage's compound and awaiting restoration.

A well-cared-for 1964 Austin Mini Cooper bought for £200 and a bottle of wine in 1979 and then fitfully restored over the next sixteen years. The suspension is dry and the wheel trims are Cooper S.

The famous Crayford badge designates this Cooper as a Mini Sprint, a high quality '60s convertible.

(Right) Mini Sprint with its substantial mohair hood erected and detachable sliding side windows in place.

(Below) Believed to be the only running example in the UK, this concours winning Crayford Cooper Sprint example belongs to Clive Powell and has been painstakingly restored after he acquired it in 1990.

This is a Portuguese production Californian prototype Mini Moke designed to show what the 1989 specification model would look like. It has covered just 5,000 miles (8,045km) and belongs to former Rover director Malcolm Harbour.

This immaculate and concours winning 1980 Clubman 1275GT belongs to Kate Perrins. Bought as an MOT failure this Clubman has been completely rebuilt by Kate with help from her friends.

(Below) Minis ready for racing on a sunny summer afternoon at Snetterton.

anticipate will eventually become almost universal for saloons of all sizes.'

Their first choice as a rival was in their view the archetypal compact car, the Mini, in Clubman Estate form. This was joined by the Fiat 127, a Datsun 100A Estate and a Sunbeam Sport, the performance variant of the Hillman Imp. In their summing up, *Motor* were painfully accurate in their assessment. 'Regrettably, the Mini Clubman estate is easily disposed of. As a package, it is still unrivalled. It is easily the most compact car of the five, yet has plenty of interior space, so if you have a particularly small garage or the constant need to park in confined spaces then the Mini is for you, especially as it is one of the cheapest cars in the group. Unfortunately in most other respects it is also the worst car in the group, with the poorest performance, gear change, ride and road holding. It's the sad result of some 10 years of neglect.'

Two years later, in 1975, *What Car?* had what they believed were the answers to the energy crisis as cheap and basic transportation. The Clubman was pitted against the cheap and cheerless Lada 1200 Estate and the Renault 4DL. The magazine believed that there was a market for these cars despite the popularity of the hatchback. The Clubman did not impress: 'The Mini Clubman's carrying capacity will satisfy those people whose demands are not excessive. It is a light, easy to drive, economical car that provides basic transport at an inflated price (£1,248).' The winner turned out to be the Renault, which the magazine admitted was an emotional as well as practical decision. The Mini was outclassed by a Renault and a Lada – what a sad state of affairs!

Given the continuing success of the Mini and the benefit of hindsight, maybe BL should have retro-fitted the Mark III front end, dusted off their woodwork tools and carried on marketing the smallest estate. It could have been a contender in the 1990s; currently the classic woody is the most popular classic Mini variant, apart from the original Cooper. Surely it is not too late to bring it back?

THE GLIMMER TWINS – RILEY ELF AND WOLSELEY HORNET

Badge engineering was almost a religion among car manufacturers in the 1950s and 1960s. As marques merged and models were rationalized, it still seemed sensible to cultivate marque loyalty; certainly plenty of customers would buy a car simply because it had a certain badge on the bonnet. As Bill Preston (now Sales Director, then salesman at G. Kingsbury, BMC dealers in Hampton, Middlesex) remembers: 'Wolseley was the popular choice around here. The only car with its name in lights our affluent, upper middle class customers preferred to be seen in a Wolseley. So for us badge engineering was a very good thing.'

BMC were delighted that the spin-offs from the original ADO 15 had all been incredibly successful. Having cornered the basic transportation market with the Austin and Morris Minis, dominated the small commercial sector with the van and pick up then gone on to create huge demand for a sports saloon courtesy of the Cooper, the only way was up. Hence the pocket-sized Rolls Royce look in the shape of the Riley Elf and Wolseley Hornet. And what shapes they were too; not content with an interior that resembled the smallest room in a stately home, BMC also made an effort to give the cars highly distinctive body styles. These models were not just cynical badge engineering exercises, they were a little different, often embracing developments that would eventually filter down through the rest of the range.

The man behind the re-style was Dick Burzi, who had worked on many of the 1950s Austins. Consequently the styling was a retrograde step. The clean, simple lines of the original car were compromised in the interests of gentrification. At the back there were little fins, despite the fact that these were rapidly going out of fashion. The intention was to add authority to the rear end and provide a better frame for the more traditional boot, though the 6cu ft (170 litres) of space only amounted to a 9 per cent increase in capacity over the standard saloon. Although it could accommodate slightly more bulky items, the lid was hinged at the top and the number plate was not hinged at all – so any luggage overspill could not be piled conveniently on top of the lid. Parking was also more of a problem as the fancy tail added 8.5in (216mm) to the overall length.

The launch Elf had rear wings, a fancy grille and lots of chrome. The Wolseley Hornet was identical on the outside except for dummy radiator. Within months both models had bumper overriders and a diagonal seam on the front wing like all other Minis.

At the front there was an equally preten-tious upright grille arrangement, which amounted to a 1930s throwback, with exag-gerated moustache chrome addenda at either side. Worst of all, the grille was attached to the bonnet. Access to the engine was always limited at the best of times, but this great big chrome tooth just got in the way.

Practicality was therefore not the models' strong point, but according to the BMC

Riley Elf/Wolseley Hornet Mark I (October 1961 to November 1962)

Engine

Type	Four cylinder in line; cast iron block transversely mounted in front
Capacity	848cc
Bore and stroke	62.94mm × 68.26mm
Output	34bhp at 5,500rpm
Compression ratio	8.3:1; automatic 9:1
Maximum torque	44lb.ft at 2,900rpm; automatic 44lb.ft at 2,500rpm

Transmission

Type	Front-wheel drive
Gear ratios	4-speed 3.765/5.317/8.176/13.657 13.657 (reverse) (final drive)

Suspension

Front	Wishbones, rubber cones, Armstrong dampers
Rear	Trailing arms, rubber cones, Armstrong dampers
Steering	Rack and pinion

Brakes Hydraulic drum/drum

Tyres/Wheels 5.2in × 10in cross-ply/3.5in × 10in

Dimensions

Track (front)	47.375in (1,203mm)
Track (rear)	45.875in (1,165mm)
Wheelbase	80.16in (2,036mm)
Length	128.75in (3,270mm)
Width	55in (1,397mm)
Height	53in (1,346mm)
Unladen weight	1,393lb (632kg)
Fuel capacity	5.5 gallons (25 litres)

Performance

Top speed	73mph (117kph); automatic 70mph (113kph)
Acceleration	0–60mph in 32.3 seconds
Fuel consumption	40mpg (7 litres per 100km); automatic 33mpg (8.5 litres per 100km)

Production

Riley Mark I	3,522
Wolseley Mark I	3,166

---

research, owners of Elfs and Hornets were the least likely to tinker with or overload their little limousines. They also did not plan on going anywhere too fast, the extra few pounds of weight and reduced aerodynamics meant that the 848cc engine had a slightly harder and slower time of it.

MINI LIMOS LAUNCHED

As a triumph of snobby style over practical content, the Elf and Hornet were completely successful. The differences between the standard and these swish minis was obvious when they arrived in the market in October 1961. Apart from the revised face and tail, the join between the A panel and front wing was missing. There was a smooth line from headlight to door hinge, which would not last for long. The bumpers were different too: they had no overriders and at the back they were a full wraparound design. The grilles were in keeping with the marque identities as the more upmarket and slightly more expensive Riley had a peaked and blue badged affair, while the Wolseley featured its illuminated name. Chrome trim also decorated the windscreen and bonnet join and ran around the side on to the door and finished at the C pillar. Cooper style surrounds also perked up the side windows and there were of course full De Luxe wheel trims, with the option of whitewall tyres. Colours were unique to the range and often featured a contrasting roof.

Inside, the Elf and Hornet were a class apart from the standard Mini and even maintained a little respectful distance between themselves. The Elf was regarded as the hierarchical leader so it had a full width walnut dashboard with a lockable glove compartment on either side of the three instrument dials. By contrast, the Hornet had the standard oval three-instrument binnacle with a wood veneer finish. Otherwise, both cars had increased seat padding, the facings being leather cloth, and extensive carpeting.

George Bishop, editor of *Small Car*, had some reservations when he first tested a Riley Elf in September 1962. 'Heads turn when you drive an Elf. People recognize it as some rich relation of the BMC twins, but are puzzled by the boot at the back, the chrome waistband and the cloud of cigar smoke around it ... the traditional Riley radiator shell that lifts up with the bonnet, all ready to bang your head on ... at the rear it has a boot with six cubic feet capacity which will take many odds and ends or one large suitcase and fewer odds and ends ... The Elf, a creature which surely should be light and airy, is in fact 190lb heavier than a standard Mini ... the boot lid is decidedly heavy to lift and, by the way, ready to snap down like a Zambesi crocodile on the unwary.' Even so Bishop was not put off completely, 'I liked the Riley, and had a great deal of fun driving it ... The finish is better than on the cheaper Mini versions, and the interior with better seats, carpets and all that wood and leather-like stuff, is cosier.'

MARK II

Development of these luxury cars was fairly rapid. BMC were quick to appreciate that nothing but leather trim would do, so this was made standard in 1962. The prominent body seams, which had been expensive to engineer out of the original model, were now an integral part of the structure, while the bumpers were beefed up with overriders.

They also addressed the sluggish performance the following year with the launch of the Mark II models, which featured a new

Inside an Elf with its full dashboard incorporating two huge glove compartments.

By contrast, the Hornet's interior was positively stark with the three instrument binnacle from the Super Deluxe adorned with veneer.

998cc engine. It consisted of an Austin/Morris 1100 block and the shorter-stroke crankshaft from the Morris Minor. The extra 4bhp made a difference to both the speed and economy, while a wider front brake and twin leading shoes made stopping a formality.

MARK II REVIEWED

Motor were pleased to see the improvements featured on a Wolseley Hornet and pronounced that although it 'costs over £100 more than the basic Mini ... the trappings of luxury ... put it in a small but useful market of its own.'

As with most of the Mini range, Hydrolastic suspension was fitted in 1964. *Small Car* – which had now become *Car* with Doug Blain at the helm – still had plenty against the upmarket version of the Mini. Given a Hydrolastic Wolseley to play with, this is what he said: 'Pitch free ride on wavy and

bumpy surfaces is supposed to be Hydrolastic's forte, and certainly in the BMC 1100 range and even more in the 1800 there's an astonishing freedom from vertical movement even on the most frightful farm tracks. The Hornet's short wheelbase does not really make such an ideal platform, and at the fairly high cruising speeds of which the car is capable a sensitive driver gets the feeling that there isn't really time for the front end to warn the tail accurately about what's coming ... The less said about the Wolseley part of the specification the better; the hideous grille on the front is a mere mockery (it is more than two feet away from the radiator proper anyway) and the ungainly bustle at the back makes just enough difference to the overall length to keep the car out of the special little parking spaces which so often seem to open up for an ordinary Mini.'

Just in case their readers did not get the message, the magazine returned to the same theme in June 1966 when they compared the

The finned rear end was meant to add class and a tad more luggage space (0.5cu ft to be precise) to the Wolseley Hornet. Seen here at the 1961 Earls Court Motor Show.

Riley Elf/Wolseley Hornet Mark II and III
(February 1963 to October 1966 to August 1969)

Engine

Type	Four cylinder in line; cast iron block transversely mounted in front
Capacity	998cc
Bore and stroke	64.6mm × 76.2mm
Output	40bhp at 5,250rpm
Compression ratio	8.3:1
Maximum torque	52lb.ft at 2,700rpm

Transmission

Type	Front-wheel drive
Gear ratios	4-speed 3.765/5.317/8.176/13.657 13.657 (reverse) (final drive)
	Optional 4-speed automatic from October 1967

Suspension

Front	Wishbones, rubber cones, Armstrong dampers; Hydrolastic from September 1964
Rear	Trailing arms, rubber cones, Armstrong dampers; Hydrolastic from September 1964
Steering	Rack and pinion

Brakes   Hydraulic drum/drum

Tyres/Wheels   5.2in × 10in cross-ply/3.5in × 10in

Dimensions

Track (front)	47.375in (1,203mm)
Track (rear)	45.875in (1,165mm)
Wheelbase	80.16in (2,036mm)
Length	128.75in (3,270mm)
Width	55in (1,397mm)
Height	53in (1,346mm)
Unladen weight	1,477lb (670kg); Mark II 1,465lb (665kg)
Fuel capacity	5.5 gallons (25 litres)

Performance

Top speed	77mph (124kph)
Acceleration	0–60mph in 24 seconds
Fuel consumption	35mpg (8 litres per 100km)

Purchase price

Hornet	£633
Elf	£654

Production

Riley Mark II	17,816
Riley Mark III	9,574
Wolseley Mark II	16,785
Wolseley Mark III	8,504

Hornet to a Hillman Super Imp. In the all important areas of handling and performance the Hornet came out decidedly on top. Otherwise the car's styling and the fact that there was no synchromesh on first gear counted against it. Obviously *Car* lost no opportunity to rubbish the Hornet's pretensions. 'Both the Wolseley and the Hillman are wrong insofar as they pretend to be luxury cars. They are too small to be truly luxurious and still hold four people. With this in mind, we prefer the Hillman because it is much less false: it lacks the Hornet's silly associations with a long-dead marque, and it offers a few more genuine features such as sound deadening. The other things are valuable only when they help to disguise any economy car's bargain basement origins. In fact the only luxury to which either aspire is psychological.'

MARK III

In October 1966 the model entered its final Mark III phase and some important Mini firsts. The most immediately apparent change was that the door hinges were now internal. Inside, both driver and passenger could gracefully wind down the windows, rather than crudely slide them open. If that was not enough, ventilation entered a new era with eyeball type vents mounted at either end of the dashboard. Even changing gear became a pleasure thanks to the Cooper remote gear change.

However, the days of the Mini limousine were numbered, although there were continuing subtle changes to the specification. More comfortable re-styled seats, along with another Mini first in the shape of a combined stalk switch on the steering column, were

Mark III Hornet on the Embankment, London, pictured in its last year of production, 1969.

introduced in 1967. This was the year when an automatic gearbox finally became available as an option. Nevertheless, rational Leyland saw no room for these most niche of niche products. Yet surely keeping at least one upmarket version in production would have been one way to claw back some profit on the Mini? A premium model always makes premium profits and the Hornet and Elf were a consistent sellers, so it seems odd that the models were dropped – but then, Leyland spiked the Cooper too.

MILITARY MINI MOKE

The Mini Moke episode is a confusing and ultimately disappointing tale. Officially sold as part of the Mini Commercial range throughout its production life in Britain, it was never that commercial (or even that practical, especially when it came to making its mark in the UK) and was destined to flourish elsewhere.

On the face of it, it seems to been incredibly optimistic of BMC to think that they could build a military vehicle based on the Mini. However, during the Second World War, when he was working for Morris, Issigonis had designed a 'mini' tank, the Salamander. This was a scout car of monocoque construction; its torsion bar suspension was later used on the Morris Minor while the front wheel drive and wishbone suspension would surface many years later on the Mini and indeed the Moke. Not only that, Issigonis had been involved in the development of the Austin Champ, a Rolls Royce powered four-wheel-drive that never came close to rivalling the Army's abiding Land Rover preference.

Issigonis had been doodling an open vehicle for some while during the development of the Mini and had prototypes running at the same time. Certainly, BMC liked the idea of a big juicy War Office contract. There was a

need for a small light vehicle much like the original Willys Jeep that could be parachuted, packed flat and generally abused. Indeed, the Royal Navy had been using Citroen 2CV pick ups built in Slough specifically for the Admiralty. These pick ups were hoisted up by helicopters and dropped ashore for operation over rough terrain. Production of these was coming to an end, so there was potentially a large military market.

Unfortunately, the prototypes prepared by BMC did not quite measure up. They were incredibly light at under 3 cwt, hardly surprising as they were made from buckboard with Mini suspension and a 948cc A series engine. These Mokes passed the stacking test with flying colours, but were disappointing when it came to anything approaching off-road work. Tiny ground clearance hampered their terrain-hopping abilities. Gradients were a problem, and the buckboard was hardly tough enough – back to the drawing board. What Issigonis came up with in 1962 was a shorter wheelbase at 72.5in (1,842mm); he also raised the suspension and stuck a sump guard under the engine in an attempt to tackle the lack of ground clearance. It now had the name 'Moke' – apparently Australian slang for a donkey – but that did not help.

You certainly cannot accuse BMC of giving up easily, as Issigonis now proposed going to four wheel drive by installing an 848cc A series engine at the rear of the vehicle. This was quickly referred to as the Twini Moke and dramatically overcame the traction and performance problems suffered by the original prototype. Novel as this solution was, it failed to impress the authorities.

CIVVIE MOKE

After getting the thumbs down from the military, BMC now tried their luck with the civilian population. Having invested so

The Mini Moke.

(Right) *BMC never gave up the idea of a military vehicle and produced the Twin Moke, seen here on snowplough duties sometime in 1970. Although obviously fun, it had little potential.*

much time and effort to get this far, the next stop was the home market and some subtle changes to make it saleable. They reverted to the standard Mini wheelbase, 848cc A series engine, sub-frames, steering, suspension and brakes. Using those components as the basis they built a simple steel body at Longbridge. This unitary construction vehicle succeeded in looking like the utility vehicle it was intended to be and was finished in smart military Spruce Green paintwork.

The front end was flat, featuring a stamped-out grille with headlamps and large indicators. The bumper comprised a simple steel bar. At the side were boxy sills, almost like raised running boards, which contained extra storage space as well as the battery and fuel tank. At each end of these sills were substantial, flat mudguards. The equally flat screen could fold flat and be detached, just like the bonnet, the most curved item of metalwork anywhere on the vehicle. At the back was more flat steel, and in traditional off-roader style a spare wheel was mounted on the panel. Inside, there was a single driver's seat; any others were optional extras. Like the saloon, it had a single central instrument pack, but there the similarities ended. The speedometer was placed in a bulkhead-mounted pod with switches and ignition sited at each corner.

Austin/Morris Moke (October 1964 to October 1967)

Engine
Type	Four cylinder in line; cast iron block transversely mounted in front
Capacity	848cc
Bore and stroke	62.94mm × 68.26mm
Output	34bhp at 5,500rpm
Compression ratio	8.3:1
Maximum torque	44lb.ft at 2,900rpm

Transmission
Type	Front-wheel drive
Gear ratios	4-speed 3.765/5.317/8.176/13.657 13.657 (reverse) (final drive)

Suspension
Front	Wishbones, rubber cones, Armstrong dampers
Rear	Trailing arms, rubber cones, Armstrong dampers
Steering	Rack and pinion

Brakes   Hydraulic drum/drum

Tyres/Wheels   5.2in × 10in cross-ply/3.5in × 10in

Dimensions
Track (front)	47.375in (1,203mm)
Track (rear)	45.875in (1,165mm)
Wheelbase	79.9in (2,029mm)
Length	120in (3,048mm)
Width	51.5in (1,308mm)
Height	56in (1,422mm)
Unladen weight	1,176lb (533kg)
Fuel capacity	6.25 gallons (28 litres)

Performance
Top speed	65mph (105kph)
Acceleration	0–60mph in 22 seconds
Fuel consumption	33mpg (8.5 litres per 100km)

Purchase price   £405

Production
Austin	5,422
Morris	9,096

A switch operated just one windscreen wiper, a second being an optional extra. At least the occupants could stay dry, thanks to a vinyl-treated fabric hood supported by poles placed around the deck. Side screens and a heater, though, were on the extras list.

This open-top utility Mini was launched in January 1964 as the Austin Mini Moke.

The only significant mechanical differences from its hardtop cousin were a higher 3.44:1 final drive, a revised gear ratio and ignition timing designed to cope with poor grade petrol. The Morris version arrived six months later and badging was the only difference. The most attractive thing about this new vehicle was its price. As a commercial vehicle there was no Purchase Tax and it had a bottom-line price of £405.

It was no surprise that the re-classification of this vehicle in 1967 as just another passenger car added £78 and killed off the plucky little Moke. In truth, it was the poor relation of the range – never updated, revised, or deemed appropriate for Hydrolastic conversion. As the Army discovered, the Moke never fitted easily into the work sphere because of the low power and negligible ground clearance. It stood more of a chance as a purely recreational vehicle, but as the British climate was hardly ideal to experience completely open air motoring the bulk of production went abroad.

MOKE REVIEWED

The Moke was largely ignored by the British press, and *Motoring Which?* probably best summed up the general apathy surrounding this unusual vehicle. 'You have to accept the fact that the Moke is not a car for long journeys. Once you have accepted that, the Moke is fine if it's fine, and not if it's not. Unfortunately, it suffers by not being as cheap as it looks. If you want a cheap country workhorse, the basic Renault 4 at £544 seems a much better bet. And in town, unless you are very optimistic about the weather, it does seem slightly eccentric to pay nearly as much as a Mini for a car which gives you such an unpleasant time in bad weather. If you can afford to keep a Moke tucked away to enjoy the fine weather when it comes, well

and good. Otherwise we would think that you are likely to spend more time being miserable in the Moke than being happy. But we hope that BMC are making a fortune exporting it to San Francisco.'

What the Moke did provide was an excuse for magazines to do pseudo Swinging London photo spreads. *Car Magazine* sent their 'kinkiest staffer' Jan Condel to try the Moke for size and found that 'It mayn't be much in the mud – but in Chelsea it is fab, gear, rave.'

Despite all the practical criticism, conversion specialists Crayford saw the trendy potential and produced a Surrey version with a striped roof and trim. When it was picked up by the producers of the television series *The Prisoner* it made quite an impact. Its film career also included guest appearances in the Beatles film *Help!* and in the James Bond film *The Man with the Golden Gun*. So maybe more shrewd marketing at the time would have helped the car's fortunes.

The Moke story did not end in 1968 when production had topped 14,500 (although only 1,500 had been sold in the UK). Subsequent chapters were set in Australia, Portugal and Italy.

It has also made several comebacks to Britain over the years. Runamoke, the Moke specialists based in London, imported Australian-built Mokes in the late 1960s and 1970s complete with huge bedstead-like kangaroo bars. In 1983 Austin Rover asked for tenders for the UK Moke franchise and Dutton Cars won. These 998cc models with an Australian/Californian specification included 13in spoked wheels, roll cage, additional bumper bars, high back seats and hood. Due to import restrictions and other difficulties only around a dozen examples were sold. Things went a little more smoothly for the Duncan Hamilton group, which successfully imported Mokes from 1988 until Portuguese production ceased in 1993.

8   Blunt Front – Clubman

'Oh my poor Mini! What have they done to you?'

John Bolster

The Mini was perfect. So why tamper with perfection? But tamper they did, and the result was the Mini Clubman. If anything looked as though it had been designed by a committee then it had to be the Clubman. BL needed to make more money from their small car and ideally replace it. Indeed, the Wolseley and Riley derivatives had proved that you could charge more if there was enough chrome and equipment to justify a price hike.

'First of all they have ruined the appearance, which is a great pity because the original car was completely functional and well proportioned. That awful Clubman bonnet would look very well on a Japanese car, but it clashes hopelessly with the shape of the rest of the body. In any case it's less efficient aerodynamically than the original bonnet and probably takes a mile or two off the top speed. They have also stuck boy racer stripes along the sides: just the thing to attract the attention of the police.' So wrote a very disappointed John Bolster for *Autosport* about his 1275GT.

FORD CLUBMAN

Roy Haynes – a designer previously with Ford as head of Car and Truck styling and the BMH shell-making subsidiary Pressed

Steel Fisher – was given a brief to come up with a re-styled body for the Mini. With the Cortina Mark 2 to his credit maybe it was not surprising that Haynes should come up with a squared off bonnet just like contemporary Cortinas. He also tacked on a sizeable rear end and huge C pillars, with no suggestion initially that it could accommodate a third door. Although the rear flange gave a natural break for a hatchback, the hump itself still looked very unnatural indeed. Another route explored by Haynes in his search for extra luggage space was to utilize the winged rear end from the Elf and Hornet. It got as far as a mock-up before being rejected. So Leyland ended up using only the front end. This made the Clubman 4in (102mm) longer than the Mini 1000, a touch heavier at 1,406lb (638kg) and less economical too at 34mpg (8.3l/ 100km) instead of 35mpg (8l/100km).

And then there was the 1275GT. It had the impossible job of taking over from the much loved Mini Cooper. It had three years to establish a reputation before the Cooper S was phased out, but dismally failed to leave any lasting impression. There was more Ford influence too, with the smallest Rostyle wheels yet, looking like those used on the Cortina 1600E. Even the 1275GT decals aped those running down the side of the hugely impressive GT40.

Despite all these obvious objections the Clubman never suffered that badly in the market, even though at £720 the saloon cost £45 more than the standard 1000. The buying public simply lapped up any new version of the Mini. The flat, square bonnet was relieved by just a few ridges leading down to a snub front that housed a full width grille with round headlamps at either end and a chrome trimmed grille. The bumper was much higher and the new grille badge formed a narrow centrepiece. It was like seeing an

(Above) So-called 'Barrel Phase' prototype. Note the family resemblance to the 1800 range.

Inside, the Clubman driver got the instrumentation directly in front of the steering wheel in a little plastic box, a radical break with the centrist Mini instrument tradition of the previous decade.

old and handsome friend after some ill-advised plastic surgery, and the front end still looks just like the afterthought it was.

At the time, though, it was different enough to be interesting and the interior updates were worthwhile. Kate Perrins, whose 1275GT was photographed for this book, does not have a problem with the nose. 'There is four inches more room under the bonnet, it makes all the jobs under there easier. My engine, which is prepared to concours standard, would not be as good if it was in the tight bay of a Cooper. For me, the Clubman is much more practical and easier to look after.'

The Clubman came with essentially the same level of trim as the Super De Luxe Mini, but was distinguished by the door trims and an innovative instrument binnacle that sighted the two dials directly in front of the driver: the speedometer on the left and a combined fuel and temperature gauge on the right. A three-spoke steering wheel with 'Clubman' on the boss was another original feature. The thickly padded seats were more comfortable too, so it was not all bad news. Another significant gain was fresh air ventilation, provided by the extremely efficient and brilliantly simple eyeball vents so popular in the 1960s. Overall, the interior had a distinctly Ford aura, not least because another ex-Ford stylist, Paul Hughes, designed it. In particular, those air vents were just like the 'Aeroflow' system on the Cortina. And atop the now padded dashboard, a D-shaped revolving ashtray was very similar to that enjoyed by the rear seat passengers in a Ford Anglia. Then there was the three-spoke, deep-dished steering wheel on the 1275GT, again reminiscent of the Cortina. (BL were not bothered, as they signed off ADO 20 and set about reorganizing the company. Haynes left amid the chaos, when his dream of streamlined model ranges was unlikely to happen.)

While the standard Minis had switched back to rubber cone suspension, the Clubman retained the expensive Hydrolastic system until 1971. Under the bonnet was the 998cc engine and, as on the standard Mini, automatic transmission was extra. Across the range an Estate version directly replaced the Countryman and Traveller, while the 1275GT was seen as the logical successor to the current Cooper.

The Mini Clubman with fashionable models in an upmarket Swiss setting. Just the image BL were after.

Mini Clubman (March 1969 to August 1980);
Mini Clubman Estate (October 1969 to August 1980)

Engine

Type	Four cylinder in line; cast iron block transversely mounted in front
Capacity	998cc (Estate 1,098cc from October 1975)
Bore and stroke	64.6mm × 76.2mm/83.73mm
Output	38bhp at 5,250rpm; 40bhp at 5,100rpm from June 1974 (automatic 41bhp at 4,850)/45bhp at 5,250rpm
Compression ratio	8.3:1; automatic 8.9:1/8.5:1
Maximum torque	52lb.ft at 2,700rpm; 51lb.ft at 2,600 from June 1974/56lb.ft at 2,700rpm; automatic 52lb.ft at 2,750rpm

Transmission

Type	Front-wheel drive
Gear ratios	4-speed 3.765/5.317/8.176/13.657 13.657 (reverse)
	4-speed automatic (not estate)

Suspension

	Hydrolastic to June 1971, then rubber cones
Steering	Rack and pinion

Brakes

Hydraulic drum/drum (two circuits from September 1977)

Tyres/Wheels

5.2in × 10in cross-ply/3.5in × 10in

Dimensions

Track (front)	47.375in (1,203mm)
Track (rear)	45.875in (1,165mm)
Wheelbase	80.2in (2,037mm) – Estate 84.18in (2,138mm)
Length	124.6in (3,165mm) – Estate 134in (3,402mm)
Width	55.5in (1,410mm)
Height	53in (1,346mm) – Estate 53.5in (1,359mm)
Unladen weight	1,406lb (638kg)/1,424lb (646kg) – Estate 1500lb (680kg)
Luggage capacity	5.5cu ft (156 litres); 4.1cu ft (116 litres) from 1974
Fuel capacity	5.5 gallons (25 litres)/7.5 gallons (34 litres)

Performance

Top speed	74mph (119kph)/82mph (132kph)
Acceleration	0–60mph in 21/17.9 seconds
Fuel consumption	34mpg (8.3 litres per 100km)/37mpg (7.6 litres per 100km); automatic 33mpg (8.5 litres per 100km)

Purchase price £720

Production 275,583

CLUBMAN REVIEWED

The press reaction to the first – and so far only – major stylistic change to the Mini was generally enthusiastic. *Custom Car* wrote colourfully about the new model. They reckoned that the Elf and Hornet were wrong turns that deviated too far from the spartan original, but 'All they needed to do was refine the basic formula to pamper to the buyers who feel they've got something a bit better than Glad and Bert's six year old 850 ... and pull back some of the doubters who maybe thought that buying a ten-year-old design did not adequately reflect their automotive trendiness.' Consequently they like the wind-up windows, new dashboard and extra elbow room under the bonnet. 'Not, then a truly memorable little car, but not half as bad as some pundits would have us believe.'

Motor also liked the new package and tested all versions in October 1969. 'Many of our criticisms have been answered in one go with the introduction of the long nosed variants which are a lot more civilized and habitable than any previous Mini. The much improved seats point to a growing awareness within the Austin Morris division of British Leyland that seating comfort really matters. Add to this the significant changes in the ventilation, furnishings and instrument layout, not to mention the all-synchromesh gearbox introduced earlier and a gear change that feels much better than before, and the result is a dramatic overall improvement in both creature comforts and drivability. No longer is a long Mini journey something of an endurance test, even though the noise level is still high (particularly so in the 1275GT) when the engine is extended and the ride on poor roads as bouncy as ever.'

One serious proposal in 1973 was widening the Mini – inserting 8in (203mm) into a Clubman for extra elbow room. Unfortunately, the cost of making a Maxi-Mini (there is a close frontal resemblance) was prohibitive. Adding length was far cheaper than adding width, which would also seriously affect fuel consumption.

During its eleven-year production run the Clubman changed very little. Like the standard Mini there was not much money to throw around on development during the 1970s. Broadly, the mechanical modifications were as the Mini. June 1971 must count as one of the most significant dates, when suspension on the saloon was switched to rubber cones. In 1972, improved synchromesh made gear changing easier and an alternator did the same for battery charging. Radial ply tyres arrived in 1973 along with rod-shift gear change. For 1974 it was inertia reel seat belts, heated rear window and twin silencer exhaust. An important adoption in 1975 was the 1,098cc engine for the manual gearbox saloon – a unit first fitted to the 1100 series in 1962. Consequently the manual 998cc unit was deleted and this engine was now available only with an automatic gearbox. Cloth and reclining seats were also made standard.

What turned out to be the Clubman's only major facelift came in 1976 and amounted to little more than a new grille with two chrome horizontal bars and the word 'Mini' plus the BL logo in the middle. Inside, there were instrumentation updates that affected the whole range including column-mounted stalks, rocker switches and larger pedals. There were moulded carpets, and the rear suspension was softened up. The last round of changes occurred a year later, with new wheel trims, a locking petrol cap, reversing lights, tinted glass and a leather-rimmed steering wheel.

1275GT – NOT A COOPER

The reasoning behind the 1275GT was simple: it was a direct Cooper replacement. Donald Stokes did not like the way that the Cooper tag apparently increased insurance premiums for all Minis. Even John Cooper suggested that if that was the case, why not remove the GT badge and use something more subtle like 'E' for 'executive' as a more credible and honest substitute? Certainly, the 1275 clearly was not a GT; when it was launched all the insurance companies said it was a Cooper in disguise so the insurance rating stayed the same.

1979 Clubman, not that different from a decade before.

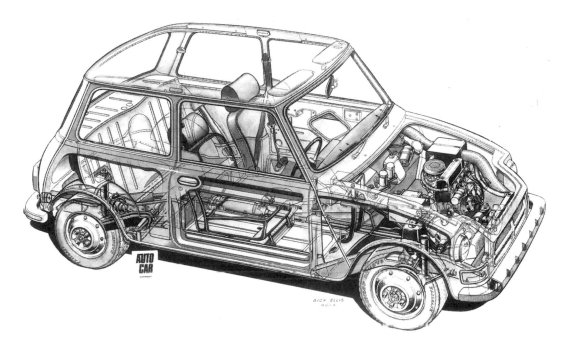

Design study for Leyland's Experimental Safety Vehicle, with lower bumpers, and a lowered front and increased impact protection.

The 'hot' Clubman was largely identical to the everyday version. The fundamental flaw was the power plant, which at 1,275cc promised Cooper S performance but could hardly deliver for a number of reasons. It was not a direct transfer from a Cooper, but from an Austin/Morris 1300. What also distanced that engine from any other Cooper credentials was the single carburettor, and the fact that both head and block were different. That added up to 59bhp as opposed to the 76bhp that a real S produced.

To address some of those problems, BL fitted a lower final drive ratio of 3.65:1, which managed to give the car a top speed of 87mph (140kph). However, the poor fuel consumption meant a return to 3.44:1 the following year. What the 1275GT did have in common with the Cooper was its front disc brakes. Otherwise they were almost unrelated apart from the fact that all the Clubmans, including the 1275GT, retained Hydrolastic suspension (as did the Cooper S until the model was discontinued in 1971).

There was one piece of equipment that the Cooper sadly missed out on, and that was a rev counter, which the 1275GT had nestling in its instrument binnacle. On the outside it was pure Clubman in shape, and only a few details picked the 1275GT out as being different. First, there was a black grille with a red GT badge on it. Other clues were the sill stripes bearing the legend 'Mini 1275GT' and the stainless steel badge on the boot. At each corner were Rostyle steel wheels looking like those used on BL's Midget sports cars and shod with radial ply tyres. Inside, apart from the three-dial binnacle, was some sporty seat trim and a leather-stitched surround on the steering wheel, which had '1275GT' on the centre boss.

Mini 1275GT (October 1969 to August 1980)

Engine

Type	Four cylinder in line; cast iron block transversely mounted in front
Capacity	1,275cc
Bore and stroke	70.64 × 81.33mm
Output	60bhp at 5,250rpm/59bhp at 5,300rpm; 54bhp at 5,250rpm from June 1974
Compression ratio	8.3:1 (low); 8.8:1 (high)
Maximum torque	69.5lb.ft at 2,500rpm/69lb.ft at 3,000rpm; 65.4lb.ft at 2,500rpm from June 1974

Transmission

Type	Front-wheel drive
Gear ratios	4-speed 3.765/5.317/8.176/13.657 13.657 (reverse) (final drive)

Suspension

	Hydrolastic to June 1971 then rubber cones
Steering	Rack and pinion

Brakes

	Hydraulic disc/drum (two circuits from September 1977)

Wheels/Tyres

Wheels	10 × 4.5in alloy/12 × 4.5in from 1974; 310mm Dunlop Denovo from 1977
Tyres	10in/145–70/Denovo 155–65SR 310

Dimensions

Track (front)	47.375in (1,203mm)
Track (rear)	45.875in (1,165mm)
Wheelbase	80.2in (2,037mm)
Length	124.6in (3,165mm)
Width	55.5in (1,410mm)
Height	53in (1,346mm); 53.55in (1,360mm) from June 1974
Unladen weight	1,476lb (669kg); 1,488lb (675kg) from June 1974
Fuel capacity	5.5 gallons (25 litres); 7.5 gallons (34 litres) from 1974

Performance

Top speed	87mph (140kph)
Acceleration	0–60mph in 14.7 seconds
Fuel consumption	35mpg (8 litres per 100km)

Purchase price   £834

Production   110,673

1275GT ON TEST

Motor tested both the Clubman and 1275GT in 1969 and used the headline, 'At last – a comfortable Mini'. Practical considerations aside, what everyone wanted to know about was the performance of the new sporting addition to the Mini stable. *Motor* found that the GT 'Has a fairly unstressed engine giving about the same output as the 998cc Cooper; so the performance is on a par with it through the gears. However, its extra torque makes it exceptionally lively in top gear, 40–60mph taking less than half the time of the present 1 litre cars, and considerably less than the old Cooper too. It compares well against its competitors, with a 0 to 60mph time of 14.2 seconds.'

Pitting the Clubman against similar cars was to become a regular pastime for the motoring press over the year, as they probed to find out how flawed the 1275GT really was. *Autocar* produced a highly detailed account of how the 1275GT measured up to the NSU 1200TT in December 1969. On performance: 'The way the Mini runs out of breath is best demonstrated by its positive refusal to reach much over 90mph even when driven flat out down a long, steep hill. This indicates how fast power falls off once you are over the peak, and why there is absolutely no point in going over 6,000rpm in road driving. The NSU, on the other hand, will cheerfully take you over 100mph if the conditions are right. There is no doubt that on a truly open road the NSU is the faster of the two cars.' Ride and handling: 'We all felt that the NSU gave a better ride than the Mini … As far as straight line stability is concerned, the Mini wins hands down.' To sum up: 'For me, the NSU wins almost every round. Yet a lot of people now thinking in terms of a 1275GT as a purchase haven't heard of the NSU, let alone given it any thought as an alternative.'

Autocar revised its opinion when the low gearing was revised: 'Performance brisk and better in every respect including economy. Rather noisy. Bouncy ride. Superb road holding and handling. Good ventilation and good fun … It is a better car than the original now performing well up around the top of its class and, being that still engagingly cheeky character of a car as any Mini, is highly enjoyable.'

A 1275GT on the move in 1973, but not moving quite as fast as a Cooper.

Perhaps the most relevant comparison test conducted during the 1970s was by *Motor* in 1974 when they took a 1275GT to France and ran it against the Innocenti Mini Cooper 1300. 'Midlands Mini, or Inni Mini?' was the headline they used. After performance testing and a 850-mile (1,368km) trip to the Dordogne and back the magazine concluded 'The Innocenti is a nicely equipped car, more powerful than the 1275GT and slightly better in ride and handling. But we feel that it does not owe much of its success abroad to superior assembly or refinement, since it retains most of the Mini's basic faults such as excessive noisiness and a basically poor ride … Certainly we were made very aware of these faults during our Continental test – we had aching backs and buzzing heads to testify to them at the end of one particularly long day's motoring – but at the same time we acquired a renewed respect for the essential excellence of the design. Long may the Mini continue.'

1275GT RUNS FLAT AND FASTER

Just like its more ordinary Clubman brother, the 1275GT changed little over the years and kept abreast of standard Mini updates. After the final drive ratio was revised in 1971, the fitting of a temperature-controlled air intake system coincided with the power output dropping dramatically to 54bhp. However, the 1275GT did have the distinction that year of being the first Mini to have 12in wheels, along with larger disc brakes and a 7.5 gallon (34 litre) fuel tank. Denovo run-flat tyres were also made an option at this time. The general Clubman facelift in 1976 resulted in the 1275GT being stripped of its GT grille badge and getting fashionably stripy seats, a vanity mirror, a second door mirror and door pockets.

In view of the many criticisms levelled at the Cooper replacement, BL Special Tuning made an attempt to liven up the 1275GT when in December 1971 they delivered a tweaked model to the offices of *Motor*. 'The standard 59bhp 1275GT only does 87.5 but, worst of all, takes 14.2 seconds to struggle up to 60, and it has been embarrassing them long enough.' The article was headed '1275GTS can it beat the old Cooper?' The car they tested was fitted with a Sport Performance Kit C-AJJ 4082, which comprised a polished head, carburettor, a mate for the existing 1.5in carburettor and a manifold to take them both, two air filters, a distributor plus a set of instructions. All the 1275GT owner needed was about four hours, some mechanical aptitude and £125. So was it quicker than the old Cooper S? 'Yes and no. Yes, it's quicker on standing starts. No, it's less tractable and slower on top speed. But there's not much in it.' The figures were impressive as the 1275GTS managed 0–60mph in 10 seconds, 0.9 quicker than the old S. The standing quarter mile (0.4km) came up in 17.4 seconds whereas the S covered the same distance in 18.2 seconds.

Overall, though, the 1275GTS was not a balanced package. Fuel consumption was an alarming 22.3mpg (12.6l/100km) during the *Motor* test and the transmission produced a 'vibro-massage' effect at motorway cruising speeds. Power delivery was hardly smooth, so it was no surprise that they gave the 1275GTS only a qualified endorsement. 'Special Tuning have added an 'S' to the badges on the boot, and there is no doubt that the car is competitive with a genuine 1275 Cooper S. Even so, it did not seem quite like the real thing to us. It was just a quick version of the 1275GT – great fun indeed but it did not satisfy our nostalgia.'

What Car? in 1977 were right when they said 'The sports car of yesterday has now virtually made way for the sports saloon of

Last of the 1275GT line has Denovo run-flat wheels and tyres as standard.

today. The mini started it in the early '60s … BMC produced their Mini Cooper.' But the market had moved on and the supermini era ushered in performance variants of popular hatchbacks. There was no Golf GTI – then only available to special order in left hand drive – but there was the Peugeot 104ZS and Renault 5TS. *What Car?* concluded that the 'Mini 1275GT is the oldest design, and it shows. Its ride is poor, accommodation marginally better than it was, but standard of finish and equipment will suit most people. Performance hardly merits the GT label. Yet the Mini has a distinct price and running advantage, and that could be important.' Although they found the Renault to be 'impressive and sporty', while 'The Peugeot 104ZS is what the Mini should be. Versatile, fast, comfortable, well

equipped and a joy to drive … The verdict must go to the Peugeot, but we wonder how it will fare when the sporty Fiestas appear. They will be good news for Ford dealers, bad for Leyland.' Those were prophetic words: Leyland entered the 1980s without a credible hot hatchback.

The last big event in the life of the 1275GT was the standardization of Denovo wheels and tyres in 1977 – presumably because British Leyland had a lot in stock. Few drivers liked them, as they provided poor roadholding and questionable run-flat ability. Creeping corporate black paint in late 1979 was splashed on the door mirrors and roof gutter, the final funeral finishing touch before the 1275GT passed away in August 1980. There was no room for the Clubman once the Metro arrived – a car that was designed to be boxy, rather than having boxiness thrust upon it.

Yet the Clubman in its day was a big success, proving that the buying public would have welcomed a more radical update to the basic model. What if the Clubman had been a bigger Haynes humpbacked hatchback? If the Clubman is to be remembered for anything, it will surely be the fact that it is the only Mini to have visibly aged.

1971 special tuning 1275GT.

Mini sports car?

In 1970 a standard 1275GT was driven to Italy and coachbuilders Micholetti. There, over two months, they transformed it into a stylish and Targa-topped two seat sports car with the project number ADO 70. It could have formed the basis of a replacement for the MG Midget. The removable roof panels predated the Fiat X/19, but it was perhaps a more comfortable cabriolet than sports car. Designer Rob Owen found out that the roof leaked quite badly on the return journey, soaking the trim and carpets. The front-wheel-drive layout, which was considered unsporting, counted against it – had they learned nothing from the Mini and Cooper?

Then there was the American problem. Rumours had been circulating for some time that the regulators were poised to outlaw open cars on safety grounds. Not only that, the tough emissions legislation would be costly and difficult for the 1275 engine to meet. So this interesting concept died, while the tired old Midget was given a supposedly new lease of life with the 1,500cc engine from the Triumph Spitfire.

Richard Bremner drove ADO 70 in September 1989 and wrote, 'Despite the extra stiffness a Targa top should lend it, there's more scuttle shake in this prototype than in the Pininfarina convertible (ADO 34). There's less go too, because it uses the weaker single carb 1275GT engine to get along. But again, you are struck by the amazing amount of room in the car, its wieldiness and sheer convenience of its size.'

9 Multilingual Minis

*'Leyland South Africa introduces the Moonlight
Mini ... the smallest and least expensive dream car.'*

Car South Africa

'World cars' has been a key phrase in the motor industry for a long time. Apparently every manufacturer ought to have a model that has global appeal, can be assembled cost-effectively by the locals and can even be adopted by them as one of their own. But the Mini has always been big abroad. Ever since it was launched, it has been completely cosmopolitan, and it has been widely exported since 1959 without interruption. Not only has it appealed to markets in all corners of the world, it has been built there too. Indeed,

at times it was the worldwide demand that kept the Mini in production during the dark days of the mid-1980s. Luckily the Japanese, French, Germans and Italians loved the Mini enough to help Rover make the decision to keep the little car in production.

Overseas Minis remained remarkably similar to British specification cars with some minor revisions to meet local regulations. For instance, Canadian and American Minis had 'bull bars', while in Chile and Venezuela the bodies were made of plastic. There were name

*The Mini is a truly global car.
This one has been modified
to comply with Canadian
legislation with higher fenders,
front and rear side indicators
and loud paintwork.*

changes too: in Denmark the Mini became the Morris Mascot while the Kombi title was applied to German estates. Inevitably they had their own special editions too: fancy an After Eight? The French did.

In Italy, Innocenti not only built their own versions of the standard Mini, Cooper and Estate, they took the concept one stage further and came up with a brand new Bertone-styled supermini. The Cooper was not just a British phenomenon, being built in several other factories across Europe long after production ceased in the UK. The Moke has also travelled particularly well, having been built in Australia, Portugal and Italy.

MINI EXPORTED

Apart from their kilometre-calibrated speedometers and left hand drive set-ups, export Minis have always been pretty close relatives of home market models. For many years models exported to Europe were badged as 'Mini Special', but this was changed to 'Sprite' in the 1990s. Occasionally these markets also benefited from a unique model that was never officially launched in the UK – like the 1300 Special, a saloon with a 1,275cc engine, which looked like a Cooper Mark III but had GT power.

In the beginning, BMC offered two levels of export trim, De Luxe and Super De Luxe, and badged cars as an Austin or Morris 850 and Super 850. A Basic and Export Saloon were added to the range in 1961 and replaced the De Luxe in 1963. The three trim levels remained for the Mark II in 1967. As the Austin and Morris names were dropped two years later the 850 Special De Luxe and 1000 De Luxe were added to the line up. The Clubman and 1275GT models were also destined for the major export markets.

Although complete knocked down (CKD) kits were sent to assembly plants around the world, some of the most fascinating, distinctive and original concepts were built at dedicated Mini production plants in many countries.

INNOCENTI

Perhaps the best known Mini manufacturer outside of the UK was Innocenti. Their models were not just re-badged and rehashed Minis, but were often thoroughly reworked and remodelled with their own distinctive character.

Founded by Ferdinand Innocenti in 1933, the company was better known for the manufacture of the Mods' favourite motor scooter – the Lambretta. However, Innocenti ambitiously began production of licence-built Austin A40s in 1960. Thus they initiated a long association with the British company, which included the Austin/Morris 1100. They also reproduced the Austin Healey Sprite and beautifully re-bodied it with coupé styling by Osi and a convertible by Ghia; production ran for ten years from 1960. If they could tackle that legendary British sports car, they could certainly take on the Mini and win.

Production of Innocenti's version of the Mini began in October 1965. Mechanical and certain body parts were imported and it was badged as the Innocenti Mini-Minor 850. The specification was British-based, with Hydrolastic suspension and virtually a De Luxe level of trim: opening rear quarter windows, lever door handles, vinyl trim, rubber mats and three-instrument binnacle. But there were side indicators mounted on the front wings, reversing lights and a distinctive nine-bar grille.

A year later the company quickly followed this up with their own version of the Cooper. It had 998cc power just like the original, but was badged as a Mini Cooper. At that

Innocenti's version of the Cooper, which continued after the UK version was dropped by BL.

Export model Mark III Innocenti Cooper to Swiss specification.

Innocenti Mini 120. Underneath the unique, hatchback body are standard A series mechanicals. The perfect marriage between Birmingham and Milan, which never officially came to the UK.

year's Turin Motor Show the company added the 'Mini t' to its range, which in English translated into estate car. Like the UK market counterpart, customers could choose between mock-Tudor timber decoration and a plain all-steel model.

The Mini-Minor went Mark II in 1968 just like the UK version, although the 848cc engine had a mild state of additional tune with its 9:1 compression ratio and HS4 carburettor producing 48bhp and a top speed of almost 85mph (137kph). The Mini Cooper Mark II came with new wheels and interior trim. It had a 9.5:1 compression ratio, 60bhp and a 93mph (150kph) top speed while the British 998cc model ran out of puff at 90mph (145kph).

Not surprisingly, the range went Mark III in 1970 with all the bodywork and trim changes first seen on the British cars in 1969. On the outside the major differences were the retention of Hydrolastic suspension and unique wind-up windows with quarterlights. Inside, it was a full-width fascia featuring five dials, with the speedometer and rev counters mounted in the middle and three minor dials in front of the driver. Italy finally got a Mini with an automatic gearbox, which was called the Mini-Matic.

After the death of Ferdinand Innocenti in 1972, BL stepped in and the new company was called Leyland Innocenti SpA. Not only did they get a new boss, Geoffrey Robinson, the whole range was renamed. The quaint Mini Minor became the much more mundane Mini 1000 and an upmarket 1001 had a timber finish on the instrument binnacle and a 51bhp engine. The Mini-Matic retained its name, while the estate got an capital T to become the 1000T. A new Mini Cooper 1300 came with UK Cooper S power and was an important revival of a charismatic name for the simple reason that the company never signed the same agreement as BMC. Apart from the badging the tyres were wider and came with wider arches that would eventually appear on UK cars. The last Cooper the company built was an Export model in 1973, with a rod gear change, dual circuit brakes, Rostyle wheels and ribbed vinyl trim.

INNOSUPERMINI

The most exciting Innocenti development during this period was the Mini 90 and 120. This was the first official hatchback-based Mini and preceded the Metro by six years. Styled by Bertone, it was a contemporary square-cut design and was perhaps one of the first Euro superminis. Underneath it all of course was standard A series Mini running gear yet it was only marginally larger than the old car – 2.6in (66mm) longer and 3.5in (89mm) wider. The Mini 90 had the 998cc engine producing 49bhp; it translated into a 87mph (140kph) top speed and was distinguished by its black bumpers. The 120 had a de-tuned 65bhp 1,275cc unit with twin carburettors, which would reach 96mph (154kph) and revelled in chrome bumpers. The only mechanical changes were a re-sited radiator (now mounted at the front) and a revised exhaust. Inside, the rear seat folded forward and despite a high loading lip offered a usefully large luggage area. The most distinctive part of the interior was the dashboard, which echoed the original Mini's central pod, though only a stylized Mini logo occupied this space, in front of the driver were rectangular cut-outs.

Cars were tested in the UK in 1975 and BL seriously considered the possibility of bringing it to their home market, especially as most of the mechanical components and some of the body pressings originated there. Plans were drawn up for a limited run of 5,000 but the company pulled out. Production costs proved to be very high and anyway the prototype ADO 88 was well under way at that time and would eventually metamorphose into the Metro. In fact, it may be a good thing that the Innocenti never came here officially. That is because all the models that were imported unofficially seemed to fall apart and then rust to bits in a very short time – thanks to low grade Eastern Block steel and Italian build quality. BL's troubles were bad enough; adding an Italian-built car to the range could have finished them off even sooner.

Their financial woes were not unconnected with Innocenti's bankruptcy in 1975. Fiat were interested in buying the company, but De Tomaso beat them to it. The standard Mini was discontinued, although Cooper production staggered into 1976 thanks to factory leftovers. De Tomaso had plans, and this included the Mini De Tomaso, based on a 120 but with a 74bhp engine. It was a very welcome mid-1970s Cooper S and headed a three car range that comprised the 90, 120 and De Tomaso. In 1982 the A series power plant was replaced by a three-cylinder Daihatsu unit to make the Mini III. That car became the Innocenti Small and in 1990 Fiat finally got their hands on the company. In 1993 the car was discontinued.

AUSSIE MINIS

It all started as just another big export market, then a CKD operation and ultimately a full production facility with a large local content. The Minis originally assembled in 1961 were 848cc cars and badged as Morris 850s. Mini Coopers came a year later, and the 1275S followed in 1965. Australia was the first market to produce a Mini with wind-up windows, in 1965. Their system bore no relation to the Elf and Hornet one-piece arrangement and featured a hinging

quarter light. This conveniently luxurious touch was even extended to the Van, which was launched that year. Otherwise Australian Minis kept abreast of UK developments by introducing Hydrolastic suspension in 1965, 998cc power in 1967, and an automatic Mini-Matic and the Mark II in 1968, although the Cooper S Mark II was not launched for another year.

To celebrate the fact that the Mini was now almost Australian – about 80 per cent local content – they launched in 1969 the Morris Mini K. The 'K' stood for 'Kangaroo' and was reinforced by a logo showing the marsupial. Power was supplied by the 1,098cc unit producing 51bhp. For 1971 the corporate nose became the Clubman one, hence the name change to Mini Clubman 1100, while the Cooper was transformed into the 1,275cc Clubman GT. One anomaly was the external door hinges; Hydrolastic suspension survived until 1973. Australia then scored another Mini first with recessed door handles.

The Morris name was dropped in 1972. So was some of the Kangaroo's local content in the shape of the 1,098cc engine, abandoned in favour of the UK-built 998cc. The company took the special edition route in the late 1970s with some quite highly specified models that had alloy wheels, metallic paint and a radio cassette. By the launch of the 1275LS, which even had 12in wheels, it was all over for the Mini in Australia.

Leyland had managed to mismanage just about every aspect of their overseas operation, let alone the UK factories. Developing the P76 saloon specifically for the Australian market had sapped their resolve and finances. As the Mini faced increasing Japanese competition it was discontinued. However, there was still one more Mini-based model left in production. A very familiar model which was in theory far better suited to the outback.

AUSSIE MOKES

Australia started producing the Moke under licence in 1966 with a 998cc engine. In 1968 optional 13in wheels meant much better ground clearance than before and the Australians embarked on a development programme. The heavily revised Mark II Moke, later named simply BMC Moke, had standard 13in wheels. Power was supplied by a locally built 1,098cc unit, which had better cooling and a revised oil filter. Cooper S universal joints, larger brake cylinder and lower final drive combined with wider tracks to improve the outback performance.

Then the Australians seriously upgraded the Moke with the limited edition Californian, a name that would endure for many years. They imported the 1,275cc engine (which produced a useful 65bhp) and installed it into a slightly more garish machine. There was more than Spruce Green on offer: the roof was a paisley patterned vinyl affair and the spare wheel had a cover. Two-speed wipers, hazards and a reversing light made this the best-equipped Moke yet. The fuel tank was also moved from the vulnerable side position to the rear – obviously the ultimate Moke, but it did not last because the 1,275cc engine could not meet local emission requirements and was deleted in 1972.

Back came the 1,098cc engine in the Moke Utility, essentially a two seater pick up model. Then Leyland decided to switch to the 998cc engine and fitted emissions equipment in 1976. The Moke was back on track when the Californian was reintroduced in 1977 with white spoke wheels, bull bars and sports steering wheel with a Californian bonnet decal. Clearly off-road chic had arrived a couple of decades early.

Moke development did not end with the Californian. In 1979 the bodywork was galvanized for the first time, which put an end to corrosion worries. Mechanically it was

The 'off-road' Mini Moke flourished in a more favourable climate and was Australia's cheapest car.

overhauled for better performance. High-back, tilting seats made it even more comfortable and new stalk controls were easier to operate. Californians had a full roll cage, the hood was improved with side screens and there were now deflector screens on the windscreen. Not only that, there was an optional 1,275cc engine. Even so, the Moke was a tired old model and coming to the end of its useful life in the Antipodes. Production was discontinued in 1981, but the Moke story did not end there; it re-started slightly closer to its original home.

PORTUGAL

Even before the Moke was cold in Australia, CKD kits had been finding their way to Setubal in Portugal. It was no accident that Mokes were ending up here because at the Industria Montagem factory owned by Leyland, building the vehicles allowed the company to sell Metros. A smart way around import restrictions was to build vehicles locally and there was nothing easier to bolt together than a Moke. So there were no big start up costs or skilled labour, and lots of profitable Metro sales. The Moke they built was essentially an Australian-specification Californian. That meant 998cc (the 40bhp engine from Britain), 13in white spoked wheels, roll cage, high back seats and zipped side screens. Some even made it back to the UK, although Dutton Cars imported no more than a handful.

Problems at the factory resulted in bankruptcy. So a new company (which was majority owned by Austin Rover), new management, a move to a new plant and a model revamp all had to work. And they did: the Moke never looked back after standard Mini running gear was fitted, including 12in wheels, disc brakes, 998cc City engine, gearbox and differential. Demand in Europe and

Far Eastern markets soared and, possibly for the first time in its life, the Moke was profitable. Once again the Moke came back to Britain, marketed very successfully this time by Duncan Hamilton Ltd. Austin Rover did not need the bother of running such a small operation, especially after Portuguese membership of the EC meant sneaking Metros into the country was no longer necessary.

Production ceased in 1989 and the whole enterprise, including the Moke name, was put up for sale. The Italian concern Cagiva, best known for building motorcycles bought the rights and re-started production of the Moke in 1991. Inevitably it was decided to build the Mokes in the company's Italian factories. Portuguese production ceased in 1993 and it seems unlikely that production will re-start in Italy. Supplies of mechanical parts from Longbridge were proving to be a problem and re-engineering it to accept other donor items proved to be very costly. The Moke seems to have run out of puff in Portugal and stalled completely in Italy thirty years after it was written off in the UK.

BELGIUM

The majority of Minis for sale in Europe were built at BL's plant in Seneffe, Belgium. The best known were the Mini Special, a standard saloon and 1,098cc Clubman engine concoctions, and the Cooper 1300 Export. Some even made it back to Britain in right-hand drive form as personal imports. The plant was closed in April 1981.

SPAIN

BMC had a Madrid-based subsidiary, Automobiles de Turismo Hispano Ingleses SA, where production of several models took place, principally based on the Morris 1100

Portuguese-produced Moke with the Australian Californian as the model. This is a prototype for 1988 production.

and MG 1300 and including some South African variants. The Mini came to the Pamplona factory in 1968. Starting with the 1275C they added the 1000E and 1000S models to the range.

A buy-out in 1969 meant Leyland Authi was the new name and a new line up of Mini models to include the 850 and 1275GT. Mini Cooper 1300s were also built there, and were very similar to the Innocenti. Production ceased in 1976 when General Motors bought the factories. A 1990s supermini is now built there – the Corsa.

SOUTH AFRICA

With one of the largest concentrations of car factories outside Europe it is no surprise to discover yet another Leyland subsidiary operating on this continent. Odd automotive concoctions were and still are a speciality in this unique market and there was nothing

odder than the sight of a standard Mark III front end with a tail from an Elf/Hornet.

Otherwise the standard engine was a 1,098cc unit in the standard or Clubman body. They also had their own version of the 1275GT called the GTS. Production finished in 1980, with the 1275E on titchy 10in steel wheels and rather frightening drum brakes.

SOUTH AMERICA

Import quotas and limited industrial resources have always meant that getting cars into this continent has been difficult. Overcoming these problems, first in Chile, involved plastic Mini bodies. Easily assembled by a local workforce, it looked similar to the original, but did not need the welding seams. It was even mooted that production could start in the UK, but the unions objected.

Rover managed to pull off the same glass-fibre trick in Venezuela with the Minicord.

10 Mini Goes Motorsport

'I thought there was something wrong with his car when I was able to overtake him; it was only then I realized how fast the Mini was on slippery surfaces. And that was my first drive in a Mini.'

Paddy Hopkirk overtaking an Austin Healey 3000 on the 1963 Monte Carlo Rally

The quintessential Mini Cooper action shot: legendary Cooper driver John Rhodes smokes the tyres at Brands Hatch in 1966.

A major part of the Mini legend is its racing history. Not only did the little car win races convincingly, there is an amusing anecdote for just about every competition it entered. The Mini's official, factory backed involvement in motorsport was relatively brief, but the 1960s were never brighter than when a Mini was mixing it with all-comers. On both road and track it was unbeatable, humiliating much larger and more expensive cars and kick-starting countless motorsport careers.

The Mini was always cheap to buy, fun to race and easy to develop. In standard tune it proved the front-wheel-drive point and led direct to the competition-honed Cooper. Best of all, the Mini has never gone away: turn up at any weekend race meeting from circuit meeting to classic rally and you are bound to find a Mini lurking in the line up and probably finishing in the top five. Other books go into much more detail about the racing exploits of the Mini and Cooper, but here is a brief history of the official works involvement.

SMALL BEGINNINGS, A30s TO 850s

Amazingly it was the old A30 and A35 that led the way in motorsport terms and proved what a small, agile, A series-powered BMC car could do. In 1956 the father and son team of Ted and Raymond Brookes won the Tulip Rally outright in an utterly standard A30. It was a good circuit car too – there are no better recommendations than owners and Formula One racers Jackie Stewart, Graham Hill and James Hunt.

BMC were characteristically slow to see the competition potential of their new small car. Despite the almost Formula 1 nature of its design – the engine, suspension and gearbox package being as one – official interest was minimal. Despite encouraging road test feedback, the chuckable, lovable nature of

the Mini was being overlooked and when parked in the Abingdon competitions department it was largely ignored. Apparently the first person to buy a Mini specifically for competition was famed circuit racer John Handley. The first day that the car went on sale he persuaded his local dealer to part with their demonstrator and promptly drove off in the direction of the Worcestershire Rally.

Works drivers Pat Moss and Stuart Turner were credited with a very early win in a minor 1959 event called the Mini Miglia organized by the Knowldale Automobile Club, although Moss was reported as saying that the Mini was too slow, while Turner thought the car particularly uncomfortable. Nevertheless, a team was entered for that year's RAC Rally. The three Minis all dropped out with the same trouble: faulty oil seals which allowed the clutch to slip despite the best efforts of service crews squirting in powder from fire extinguishers and even road grit.

Minis tackled their first international event in the 1960 Monte Carlo. It was a reasonably successful expedition, as a works team comprising TMO 559, 560 and 561 competed alongside three private entries for glory. These accident-prone cars had an eventful time: 559 collided with a private entrant, 560 was almost written off and limped home, while 561 hit a rock. Nevertheless 73rd, 55nd, 33rd and 23rd were respectable results.

The Mini recorded its first International class win in the 1960 Geneva Rally while other 850cc models went on to contest all the major events, which included an historic first in class for TMO 561 at the Alpine Rally. This car scored another class victory in the 1961 Tulip Rally, but this was to be the last year of competition for the plucky 850cc, eclipsed by the arrival of the Cooper. However, the Mini proved that despite negligible ground clearance, and tiny wheels this was a rally weapon to be taken seriously.

The Mini makes its Monte debut in 1960 in the capable hands of T. Wisdom and J. Hay. The Austin Se7en finished 55th overall whilst P. Riley and R. Jones managed a slightly better 23rd.

ENTER THE COOPER, 1962–63

Stuart Turner became the new competitions manager for BMC and not only inherited a very well run team, but was able to give the Mini, which he had initially found so uncomfortable, its big Cooper-badged break. On the team were two very talented Scandinavians, Timo Makinen and Rauno Aaltonen, and the cars were now painted in the soon to be familiar red with a white roof, so all the elements for rally success were in place.

Their first event was the 1962 Monte Carlo, which almost ended in tragedy when Aaltonen lying second crashed into a wall and caught fire. Co-driver Geoff Mabbs rescued his unconscious team mate. It was better news for Pat Moss and Ann Wisdom, who finished 26th overall, were seventh in class and scooped the Coupe de Dames. This

pairing performed even better in that year's Tulip Rally, winning it outright, the Mini's first International win. Then in 1963 a very important driver was recruited to the Mini Cooper team: Paddy Hopkirk.

The omens were good at the start of the season as the Cooper achieved third and sixth places in the Monte Carlo. This success was followed by a second and class win in the Tulip. New signing Pauline Mayman, who replaced Pat Moss, finished fourth in class. She went on in the following Trifels Rally to score a significant class win. The stunning arrival of the 1071 Cooper S was marked by a first overall win for Aaltonen and Tony Ambrose. Paddy Hopkirk, partnered by Henry Liddon, followed this up with a third overall plus a class win in the Tour de France and then fourth overall in the season's last event, the RAC.

MINI WINS MONTE, 1964–65

Not surprisingly, with a few exceptions the S was now adopted as the main car for the 1964 season. They got off to a good start too, as Hopkirk scored the Mini's most important win to date at the Monte Carlo with other team cars finishing fourth and seventh. These winning ways continued in the Tulip with another overall victory. However, the rest of the year did not go so well. The new 1275 version proved unreliable in the Acropolis Rally, although it managed a class win in the Alpine. To confuse the S issue the short-lived 970cc participated in a few events and acquitted itself very well, winning the Ladies Cup and class in the Alpine and scoring another class win in the Tour de France.

The 1965 season was busy and much better for the Coopers. They got off to a terrific start as Timo Makinen and Paul Easter overcame appalling weather conditions to take victory in the Monte. Having started their run in Stockholm they were among only thirty-five of the original 237 starters who qualified for the elimination tests. Despite sub-zero temperatures, huge snow drifts and treacherous ice, Makinen and Easter took the now famous AJB 44B to victory. They were ably supported by Hopkirk and Liddon at 26th overall, but first in class, followed closely in 27th by the Morley twins. Frozen transmissions put paid to the teams ambitions in the Swedish Rally, as all four cars retired with seized differentials.

Hopkirk was back on form for the Circuit of Ireland, which was won outright, followed by a class win in the Tulip. The Aaltonen and Ambrose partnership won the Geneva Rally, followed by the Czech and the nearby Polish event. This left Altonen in clear sight of the European Rally Championship with just two events remaining. The Three Cities Rally (Munich–Vienna–Budapest) was also a happy hunting ground for Aaltonen, which just left the RAC and a huge works entry of six Coopers, not to mention big Healeys tackling the last event of the season. A Healey

Paddy Hopkirk and Henry Liddon on the way to an historic victory in the 1964 Monte Carlo Rally.

Hopkirk and Liddon in slightly warmer climes with the unmistakable backdrop that is classic Cote D'Azur.

3000 piloted by Timo Makinen finished runner-up to Aaltonen, who was crowned European Champion. This was the first time that a British car had won the title.

PROBABLY A ROBBERY, 1966 AND ALL THAT

The BMC competitions department would never have a stranger year than 1966. Most bizarre and notorious of all was the Monte Carlo Rally. The circumstances surrounding this event are well documented but bear a certain amount of repetition and maybe understanding. It had been well telegraphed that the French would be reluctant for the British cars in general and Coopers in particular to make much of an impression on the Rally. Apparently a home win for Citröen would make a much more popular result.

The British contingent had no reason to doubt the officials' intentions when false rumours circulated that BMC had failed to homologate the Cooper S. They had in fact exceeded the 5,000 minimum by 47, but there were suggestions that the rally version of the Cooper had little in common with a stock showroom model. More worrying were the exceedingly late regulation changes by the ruling body. However, all the British teams believed that they had complied.

Never mind the great drivers, brilliant little cars and excellent mechanical back-up, a major factor in the Mini's rally success was innovative preparation. Tony Ambrose, who had joined the team in the early 1960s, pioneered the use of more detailed pace notes,

(Above) *Architects of the '60s success. Stuart Turner (with folder) talks to Timo Makinen.*

Mid-sixties interior of a works rally car. Note the servo under the dash, the speedometer reading up to 200kph and the tacho red-lined at 8,000rpm.

Monte Minis at Abingdon. From left to right, 1964 Monte winner 33 EJB, 1965 winner AJB 44B and 'disqualified' 1966 entrant GRX 55D.

which made the co-driver's role crucial. Also Stuart Turner was the first rally manager to employ reconnaissance vehicles that ran ahead of the rally to report back on conditions. The benefits were obvious and the results followed, so it was no surprise to find that the finishing order on the 1966 Monte was Makinen, Aaltonen and Hopkirk, or Mini Cooper, Mini Cooper and Mini Cooper.

But the French did not see it this way. The post-event inspection turned into an autopsy, as the officials pulled the cars apart for technical infringements. They found plenty of irregularities between the cars' specification and homologation papers, but the BMC mechanics consistently proved that the officials were wrong. Track an extra 3.5mm wide? No, the suspension had simply settled after the exertions of the Rally. Stroke too long? This was 1,275cc, not an 850cc unit. To cap it all, highly inaccurate bathroom scales were used to measure almost every component.

Almost in desperation, the officials turned their attentions to the car's lighting system, which they claimed failed to comply with French traffic laws. Apparently the mini fog lamps also had to be used as dipped beams because the headlights contained single filament halogen bulbs. Not only were the Minis disqualified, so was the fourth-placed Lotus Cortina driven by Roger Clark, which put a Citroën DS21 in first place. Appeals failed, even though there was photographic evidence that Citroën had changed their lighting system late in the event.

In Sweden Makinen suffered a broken driveshaft, and Aaltonen hit a rock and subsequently overheated, so both cars retired. On the San Remo, Hopkirk finished sixth in class while Tony Fall was disqualified for having non-standard paper air filters. Then things started to pick up. Fall and Henry Liddon won the Circuit of Ireland, Hopkirk and Crellin the Austrian Alpine Rally, and Hopkirk took a class win in the Acropolis. Fall won the Scottish Rally and followed that up with a second overall in the Geneva event. Three more major victories followed for Aaltonen on the Czech Rally, Fall on the Polish and Makinen on the Three Cities.

The usual large Mini entry for the end of season RAC included Formula 1 world champion Graham Hill piloting one of eight cars. Finishing second, fourth and fifth overall meant a 1–2–3 in their class; despite this BMC did not see the positive side and they started to restrict funds. It was hardly surprising that faced with such difficult circumstances Stuart Turner left, handing over the operation to Peter Browning, although both men were scheduled to mount the assault on the 1967 Monte Carlo Rally.

SNOW AND MUD IN 1967

In Monte Carlo revenge for the 1966 nonsense proved to be sweet, although conditions were again difficult and the rules were revamped. Only a limited selection of tyre options were available for special stages, which required the Coopers to have a substantial roof rack each. This did not stop the team posting another historic win. Aaltonen and Liddon beat off a strong challenge from a Lancia Fulvia and a Porsche 911, while the rest of the team finished sixth with the Hopkirk and Crellin pairing, tenth in the hands of Fall, 15th for the relatively new pairing of Lampinen and Wood, with Makinen and Easter at 41st position.

The rest of year was just as encouraging with six outright wins, nine class victories and plenty of high placings. There were some fresh challenges for the Mini Cooper too as BMC took their first shot at the notorious East African Safari. Aaltonen drew up a specification sheet for his car, which included fully adjustable Hydrolastic suspension, pumped-up by a rear-seat mounted device for increasing ground clearance. In addition there were a high exhaust and air intake to stop the engine taking any mud on board. Everything was strengthened, the visible signs being a massive sump guard and large handles mounted on the front wings and back of the roof to allow the car to be lifted out of any trouble. The top-mounted windscreen wiper could also be operated manually. In the circumstances, this car needed all the help it could get as torrential rain turned the event into the stickiest ever.

Rauno Aaltonen and Henry Liddon on their way to win the 1967 Monte Carlo – the last time that the Cooper won the prestigious event.

Not surprisingly, the car came to grief in a mud-filled hole and the engine gummed up.

Hopkirk achieved a long-held ambition to win the Acropolis. On home soil in the Thousand Lakes, the Finnnish driver Timo Makinen won despite having his view of the rally obscured by a bouncing bonnet, released to aid cooling. The 1967 RAC event was cancelled due to the outbreak of foot and mouth disease so the last two events were the Alpine followed by the Tour of Corsica. Although four cars started the Alpine, three retired leaving the popular pairing of Hopkirk and Crellin to battle through very foggy conditions at the end of the event to claim victory. In Corsica there were no pleasant surprises, only a series of upsets related to faulty fan belt material, which caused the belts to slip badly. They failed to cool the engine properly and caused two premature retirements. That was the end to an eventful 1967 season.

THE FINAL COUNTDOWN, 1968–69

It was clear that BLMC were still behaving like amateurs in an increasingly professional sport, as they quaintly drove to and from events while all about them took trailers. But that was only part of the problem. The Mini Cooper had had a good run, better than most; six years at the top was impressive. Now lots of other cars were not only catching up, but overtaking. To take on big budget teams like Porsche and Renault, BLMC would have to spend some serious money – money that they did not have. So the omens for 1968 did not look good and got a little worse at the Monte Carlo Rally.

To make up for its power shortfall, two single choke Weber carburettors boosted the output of the 1275 by a token 7bhp, but the update caused consternation among the French officials. Were these modified carburettors? The regulations certainly forbade it. In the end a compromise was reached whereby if a fellow competitor objected, then the Minis were out. They finished strongly, with Aaltonen, Fall and Hopkirk registering third, fourth and fifth and top three in their class.

There were eleven championship events in 1968, but the team challenged only eight of them. Although it was becoming clear that the Mini Cooper was being regularly outclassed by more powerful opposition, the results were still impressive. After a wipeout in the Flowers Rally, Belgian driver Vernaeve drove to third and a class win. Aaltonen followed up the previous year's Acropolis win with a fifth and class victory. The Scottish Rally yielded a class win. Four months later Hopkirk took one Cooper S to the TAP Rally and came away with a very creditable second place after leading for most the way.

Hopkirk was retained for one more season and works Coopers participated in just two international events in 1969. He always excelled in the Circuit of Ireland and despite experimenting with 12in wheels, suffering a misfire and some suspension problems, came in second. This was followed by the Tour de France, where fuel injection was used. Hopkirk was joined in his assault on the road rally by John Handley in another Group 2 car and Brian Culcheth in Group 1. Hopkirk finished 14th overall, but won his class, Handley went out when lying sixth, while Brian Culcheth managed a strong class second beaten by a Julien Vernaeve's privately entered Cooper S.

Leyland's official participation was virtually over, and many of the works cars were dispatched to bounce around televised autocross events in the late 1960s. For 1970 two rallies were contested in Australia. Brian Culcheth did the honours, retiring in the Southern Cross and finishing fourth in the Rally of the Hills.

RALLYING OUT OF RETIREMENT

And that was it – until 1994. Project Mini Monte Carlo was an attempt to get the car back into the rally it had dominated in the 1960s, with the same driver and navigator combination of Paddy Hopkirk and Ron Crellin. The idea was to find out just how competitive the Mini was in a modern World Championship rally. Preparing a car for Group A regulations was hardly straightforward, especially as the engine had to be a substantially standard unit, but Brigden Coulter Motorsport managed to get an engine to produce 97bhp at the wheels. Despite some electrical problems and the car's inability to finish they were still classified in the results. Philippe Camandona finished 47th overall and third in class; Hopkirk and Crellin finished 52nd overall and fourth in class. Already a popular and successful sight on numerous classic rallies, the Mini also returned to the RAC event in 1994 driven by Russell Brooks.

History was made in 1995 when Daniel Harper and Les Reger steered the Mini to its first international win since Paddy Hopkirk won the Acropolis Rally in 1967. The event was the Vauxhall Rally of Wales and the Class was A5, beating off numerous Peugeot 306s and Vauxhall Novas to take the title. But that was not the end of the Mini's rally revival: specialists Mini Sport entered two cars to challenge for the Mobil One/Top Gear RAC British Rally Championship with Daniel Harper and Les Reger in Group A and Dave Johnson and John Flynn in Group N. After gruelling rounds in Wales, Scotland, Ireland and the Isle of Man they came out winners of Group A and runners up in Group N. The Mini was back!

Hopkirk is back! He lines up with the original Monte winning Coopers, plus four 1990s Coopers to tackle the 1994 event. Hopkirk and Ron Crellin finished 52nd overall and fourth in class.

SHORT CIRCUIT – RACING MINIS

The Minis' potential for circuit racing in the 1960s would seem to be as limited as their dimensions, especially in view of the powerful cars they were up against, which included huge Jaguar saloons and American Ford Galaxies. Size did not matter, however; ability counted for so much more. On the track, Minis proved to be astoundingly quick. Cheap to buy and prepare, they provided the perfect progression from karts for a large number of Formula 1 stars who got their start in the little cars, including James Hunt and Nicki Lauda.

The Mini stayed competitive at a national level well into the 1980s. Even today it is still hugely popular as a racer; not only does it cost so little take racing for a season, but there are lots of opportunities for close competition with the popularity of one-make series like the Mini Miglia. Here are just some of the highlights from an illustrious and very long career on the track.

1960s SUCCESS

The Cooper Car Company raced Minis (which bore their own name and distinctive British Racing Green and white bonnet striped livery from 1962) with a certain amount of backing from BMC. It paid off because John Love won the British Saloon Car Championship that year. In 1963 Sir John Whitmore was the runner up to the huge Ford Galaxie driven by Jack Sears. Ralph Broad entered a modified Cooper driven by John Fitzpatrick, John Handley and Jeff May, which proved to be highly competitive. Fitzpatrick was procured to join Cooper and he finished runner-up in the 1964 British Championship and class winner for 1,300cc cars.

In Europe a Cooper tuned by Downton Engineering, with Rob Slotemaker at the wheel, won the 1,300cc class of the European Saloon Car Championship. Ken Tyrrell ran a two-car team for Cooper with Warwick Banks and Julien Vernaeve. Banks won the European title in 1964. On home ground in 1965 the Banks roller-coaster swept on. Driving for Cooper, he scored eight out of ten victories, taking the class award in the up to 1,000cc category, but was deprived of a Championship win because of a technical protest.

Ralph Broad operated on a shoestring budget but benefited from works updates to the specification, in particular tougher gearboxes. His success in Europe resulted in BMC offering him the contract to race on the Continent in preference to Tyrrell for 1965. John Fitzpatrick rejoined the team alongside John Handley and spare driver John Terry. It was not a successful season; budgetary restraints were the problem, which meant missing some races. Back home, Broadspeed Coopers often beat Cooper Coopers. BMC therefore cancelled the European agreement.

It was all change on the home team front in 1966 when Broadspeed turned to Ford, racing Anglias and then Escorts. Fitzpatrick went with him, while over at Cooper Warwick Banks went off to concentrate on single seaters and was replaced by John Handley. Engine preparation was now a matter for Downton Engineering rather than BMC. Fuel injection (which was allowed in the regulations) meant they were fast and reliable, but John Rhodes just missed the title, which was taken by Fitzpatrick. In 1968 the Cooper team retained Rhodes who was joined by Steve Neal. It was a repeat of the previous season as Rhodes finished runner-up again, but bagged the 1,300cc class.

In 1968 BMC extended its European support to British Vita who contested races in the one litre class with drivers Handley and Alec Poole. Handley won the championship class.

LEYLAND TRY RACING

The creation of British Leyland Corporation was not good news for Minis and motorsport. The rally operation was being scaled down due to the expense of contesting these events and the emphasis was being switched to rallycross and circuits. Already Cooper were dropped, although they stayed with Downton to form the Cooper-Downton-Britax team with Steve Neal and Gordon Spice carrying out the driving duties.

The outstanding problems that affected the works rally programmes were exactly the same when it came to breathing life into the racing side, with the increasingly professional approach of other factory backed teams and the fact that the Mini was now a decade old. That did not stop the Equipe Arden organization, with Spice driving, from picking up the 1,000cc class award in 1968. For 1969 the works drivers were Rhodes and Handley who benefited from the newest development: 12in wheels.

The British Leyland logo was not to be a lucky charm. Both cars were written off in accidents at the first Brands Hatch meeting. At the following Silverstone meeting things got a little better with tenth and eleventh placings, which meant fourth and fifth in class. A third and fourth at Crystal Palace saw even more improvements. Then it was on to the continent and a fifth and sixth at Hockenheim, but both cars at the Nürburgring retired before the end of the six hours with broken rear trailing arm pivots. On to the Spa, and modified Coopers failed to stay the 24 hours. Back home, the Oulton Park Gold Cup saw Rhodes, with a Weslake-tuned 1,299cc engine, trailing twelfth.

A final continental fling for the Coopers at Salzburg saw Rhodes and Handley score an impressive 1–2. Unfortunately that did not stop the factory abandoning the Cooper for competition purposes. Although the season finished well, they had found the going tough all year against entries from Cooper and the Broadspeed Fords. It did not help that concentrating on outright wins with 1,300cc category Coopers left the 1,000cc open to others, namely Alec Poole and an Equipe Arden prepared Cooper, which won the class title and

Equipe Arden Cooper S driven by Alec Poole in 1969 when he became outright RAC champion, the last works backed win.

the RAC Championship outright in 1969. Given that the BL Competitions Department were new to circuit racing and the restrictions on development due to the engine and gearbox set-up it is remarkable that the team achieved so much. But British Leyland were in no mood to be patient.

LONGMAN LEADS REVIVAL

In 1969 Richard Longman won the first motor race televised in colour in Britain driving a Downton 1300 Cooper – he fought off the attentions of a huge Ford Falcon. In fact that was just one of twenty-seven races in which he was successful that season and he loyally stuck with the Mini for another decade to find fame as an expert tuner of A series engines. When production saloon car racing was re-established in 1972 the winner of the 1,300cc class was Jonathan Buncombe with a Longman engined Cooper S.

Once the Cooper's homologation period expired, Longman turned his attentions to the 1275GT and in 1977 revived the Mini's competition credentials in national terms. BL should be given credit for helping to qualify a

number of parts including twin SU carburettors, sportier camshaft, close ratio gearbox, 12in wheels and better Dunlop tyres. Up against a Chrysler Avenger driven by Bernard Unett – who had dominated the 1,300cc class for the previous three seasons – Longman finished second, with Alan Curnow in an identical 1275GT placed third.

In 1978 Longman put the Mini back on top with an overall win in the RAC British Saloon Car Championship. Sponsored by Patrick Motors, Longman went on to fly the flag yet again in 1979 by winning the Group 1 British Saloon Car Championship with Curnow as the runner-up. A change in the minimum weight regulations meant an end to Saloon Car Championship involvement.

> Undoubtedly a key to the Clubman's success was BL's one-make 1275GT racing series, although they switched to the Metro Challenge with the announcement of the new car. Despite that, the Mini has raced on, and you can cheer a grid full of Minis at most meetings during the season at a Mini Miglia, Mini Se7en, Ministox or one of sundry other Mini Challenges.

In 1995, Daniel Harper and Les Reger steer a Mini Cooper to its first international win for 28 years.

In the Paddock at Snetterton in 1996, Mini Se7en challengers are poised to get on the track. A reassuringly familiar sight at race tracks around the UK and Europe.

Mini Cooper motorsport rollcall

Year	Type	Driver	Title
1962	997	Love	1,000cc and overall BRSCC champion
1962	997	Moss	Tulip and German Rally
1963	1071S	Whitmore	BRSCC runner up
1963	1071S	Aaltonen	Alpine Rally
1964	1275S	Fitzpatrick	1,300cc and BRSCC runner up
1964	1071S	Hopkirk	Monte Carlo Rally
1964	1275S	Makinen	Tulip Rally
1964	970S	Banks	1,000cc and European Touring Car Champion
1965	1275S	Hopkirk	Circuit of Ireland
1965	1275S	Aaltonen	Polish, Three Cities, RAC, Geneva, Czech Rallies
1965	1275S	Makinen	Monte Carlo, 1,000 Lakes Rallies
1965	1275S	Rhodes	1,300cc and 3rd BRSCC
1965	970S	Banks	1,000cc and 2nd BRSCC
1966	1275S	Fall	Circuit of Ireland, Scottish, Polish Rallies
1966	1275S	Hopkirk	Austrian Alpine Rally
1966	1275S	Makinen	Three Cities, 1,000 Lakes Rallies
1966	1275S	Aaltonen	Monte Carlo, Tulip, Czech Rallies
1966	1275S	Rhodes	1,300cc and runner-up BRSCC
1967	1275S	Hopkirk	Circuit of Ireland, Alpine, Acropolis Rallies
1967	1275S	Makinen	1,000 Lakes Rally
1967	1275S	Fall	Geneva Rally
1967	1275S	Rhodes	1,300cc and Lombank Entrants' Award
1968	970 S	Handley	1,000cc Div 1 Euro Touring Car Championship
1968	1275S	Rhodes	1,300cc Div 2 Euro Touring Car Championship and 1,300cc RAC Championship
1968	970S	Spice	1,000cc RAC Championship
1969	970S	Poole	1,000cc and outright RAC Champion

11 Formula 1 Mini – The Cooper

'Sure ... it is an ugly little pumpkin ... But in spite of all this we cannot imagine a sports car we would rather have.'

Auto

Just as one man, Issigonis, was responsible for the Mini, then the credit for the performance version can be attributed solely to one man: John Cooper. Since 1961 his name has been inextricably linked to the smallest, fastest and most charismatic car. Locating the engine behind the driver was an inspired development that won Cooper's team the Formula 1 World Championships in 1959 and 1960. This ushered in a racing car revolution, the effects of which are still being felt today. A chance meeting between the two great men in 1946 led to a life-long friendship. Cooper had taken his prototype 500 Special to compete in the 500cc and 750cc classes at the Brighton Speed Trials. Running against him

Men behind the Mini Cooper. In front is the Monte Carlo-winning Cooper S with Issigonis on the right, then chassis engineer Charles Griffin, the man himself John Cooper, tuning guru Daniel Richmond is behind an unidentified woman, then on the left there is a slightly obscured Bill Appleby, BMC's chief engine designer who was responsible for the A series.

was Issigonis in his pre-war, rubber-suspended Lightweight Special.

Issigonis always resisted any attempts to tart up, market and generally interfere with the brilliantly simple original concept. When it came to the go-faster Mini, he was initially sceptical and took some convincing. However, the Mini Cooper proved to be the most significant model of the 1960s – perhaps of the century.

RACING DRIVER'S RUNABOUT

Just as Issigonis and Cooper had crossed paths as adversaries, the former in his Lightweight Special and the latter in a 500, they also dealt professionally. Cooper was a customer of Morris Engines, which were used in Formula Junior cars. As technical director, Issigonis would regularly liaise with Cooper on engineering matters. The successful combination of BMC A series engines in Formula Junior led to Cooper running the works team and ultimately gave access to prototype ADO 15s. He took one to the 1959 Italian Grand Prix with driver Roy Salvadori, beating fellow Formula 1 star Reg Parnell in an Aston Martin DB4GT. At the circuit Ferrari's chief designer Aurelio Lampredi asked for a drive and was suitably impressed, 'If it were not for the fact that it is so ugly, I'd shoot myself if that isn't the car of the future.'

Cooper was equally bowled over. He had been searching for a decent model as a sporting saloon. He believed that there was a market for a four-seater that could match the handling and performance of the benchmark Lotus Elite. Experiments with a Renault Dauphine fitted with a Coventry Climax engine and ZF gearbox were disappointing. It was quick, but the handling of the rear-engined car left a lot to be desired.

Cooper tinkered with an 850cc (fitting an 1,100cc Formula Junior unit) and realized that the potential for a sports version was overwhelming. Both of his contracted Formula 1 drivers – Jack Brabham and Bruce McLaren – enjoyed their new toys, so Cooper reckoned that a proper production version with disc brakes and a remote gear change would be an obvious new product for BMC. Issigonis remained distinctly unimpressed, preferring to see his creation as a simple 'people's car' despite the obvious success that some rally privateers were having.

As a compromise, Issigonis referred Cooper to BMC boss George Harriman. He listened to Cooper's proposal for a homologation run of 1,000 specially tuned Minis to qualify for touring car racing. 'Take one away and do it' was Harriman's response, even though he had doubts that 1,000 could be sold. Just two weeks later he was taken for a spin in a performance Mini prototype that contained the constituent parts of a Formula Junior engine; ADO 50 was born.

COOPER CONCOCTED – THE 997

There was not much wrong with the standard Mini. At the prototype stage the original A series installation was a 948cc, which resulted in an astonishing 90mph (145kph) speed from a mere 37bhp. Cooper was at the time extracting over 80bhp for Formula Junior in competition, which might have been considered a little excessive in a road-going Mini. Even so, a racing engine would not be refined or durable enough to cope with the demands of everyday motoring.

What they did was to stroke the 848cc to 81.28mm and reduce the bore to 62.43mm, producing the first 997cc Cooper engine. Twin 1.25in SU carburettors helped to pump the power up to 55bhp at 6,000rpm. Internally the piston tops were domed, which increased the compression ratio to 9:1. The inlet valves were enlarged, as were the exhaust bores, and double valve springs were fitted to create a high-lift camshaft, while a three-way manifold got rid of the exhaust gases. To cope with the extra power the bottom of the engine was strengthened, a damper reduced the vibrational wear and an oil way was created to feed the crank and bearings. To reduce noise, a sixteen-blade cooling fan made a big difference. This new engine made much more of a din so the amount of sound deadening material was increased on the bodywork, especially around the wheel arches.

A remote gear change was regarded as essential and this was allied to longer gear ratios, while the final drive was raised to 3.765:1. To make the whole thing stop, Lockheed specially developed the smallest set of brake discs then produced. At 7in they managed to stop the 10in wheels very effectively for the time, although they would ultimately come in for criticism. Cooper himself was instrumental in persuading the company to produce them. Even the otherwise standard rear drums were modified with a pressure limiting valve.

SUPER SPECIFICATION COOPER

The Cooper was launched privately to the press on 17 July 1961; the venue was once again the Army proving ground at Chobham. At least ten cars were required, but by 10 July all that existed were piles of unassembled parts. BMC met the deadline and the Coopers were put at the disposal of several Formula 1 drivers as ultimate proof of the car's capabilities. Everyone was impressed.

Production delays meant that the car was not revealed to the public until September, badged as the Austin Se7en Cooper and Morris Mini Cooper. The Super models with the standard 848cc unit were launched at the same time. On the outside the obvious differences were the unique grilles: the Austin had eleven thin horizontal bars and the Morris seven chunkier Venetian blind style slats. Both sets of bumpers featured corner bars and chrome surrounded the door and window frames. Perhaps the most distinctive clue that these cars were something special was the famous two-tone colour scheme. The natural break for the roof panel caused by the gutters meant that

The 997 Cooper was indistinguishable from a Super De Luxe, apart from the badging. This is a 1962 997 Cooper in competition at a 1963 autocross in Somerset.

Cooper 997cc (1961–64)

Engine

Type	Four cylinder in line; cast iron block transversely mounted in front
Capacity	997cc
Bore and stroke	62.43mm × 81.28mm
Output	55bhp at 5,800rpm
Compression ratio	9:1
Maximum torque	54.5lb.ft at 3,600rpm

Transmission

Type	Front-wheel drive
Gear ratios	4-speed 3.765/5.11/7.21/12.05 13.657 (reverse) 3.44.1 (optional final drive)

Suspension

Front	Wishbones, rubber cones, Armstrong dampers; Hydrolastic from 1964
Rear	Trailing arms, rubber cones, Armstrong dampers; Hydrolastic from 1964
Steering	Rack and pinion

Brakes Hydraulic disc/drum

Tyres/Wheels 5.2in × 10in cross-ply/3.5in × 10in

Dimensions

Track (front)	47.75in (1,213mm)
Track (rear)	45.9in (1,166mm)
Wheelbase	80in (2,032mm)
Length	120.25in (3,054mm)
Width	55in (1,397mm)
Height	53in (1,346mm)
Unladen weight	1,400lb (635kg)
Fuel capacity	5.5 gallons (25 litres)

Performance

Top speed	87mph (140kph)
Acceleration	0–60mph in 18.0 seconds
Fuel consumption	27mpg (10.4 litres per 100km)

Purchase price £679

Production 24,860

Morris Mini Cooper.

a contrasting colour looked perfect. When the main body colour was blue, green, grey or yellow the roof was finished in Snowberry White (as were the steel wheels). The exception was Tartan Red bodywork, which was contrasted by a black roof.

Inside, it was essentially Super trim. This meant full carpeting, including a boot board that formed a platform over the spare wheel. The seats were covered in two-tone leather cloth while the dashboard and top rail had black vinyl on them. In the centre of that rail was a chrome lidded ashtray, but more important was the oval instrument binnacle featuring three Smiths dials: water temperature on the left, oil pressure on the right and in the middle a speedometer that was optimistically calibrated up to 100mph (160kph).

COOPER REVIEWED

Despite the fact that the car was priced at £679 – it was £25 more than the most expensive Mini, the Riley Elf – BMC were overwhelmed with orders. The press reception that greeted the Cooper was rapturous. Confirmed Mini fan John Bolster writing in *Autosport* accepted that the time was right for a Grand Touring version of the Mini. All the correct ingredients were in place, including Formula Junior experience, remote-control gear lever and specially developed brakes.

Underpinning it all was the brilliant original concept. 'When Alec Issigonis designed his revolutionary BMC baby car, it was intended to be a better form of transport for the masses. He tried to make it as safe as possible in the hands of indifferent drivers, but in achieving this he also gained an entirely unexpected result. The road holding and stability were such that the Mini and the Seven could safely out-distance more powerful cars on winding roads.' Road testing it for the magazine a few months later Bolster was still entranced by the handling qualities. 'It is the celebrated road holding which contributes most to the overall performance. We have all seen Minis in saloon car races demonstrating their high cornering power against more conventional cars. This cornering speed is certainly a little greater than that of most of their competitors. What is so remarkable though, is the phenomenal "dicing margin" that is available.'

Sports Car Graphic used the headline 'Mini-Minor becomes Maxi-Major'. They got a sneak preview of a prototype and raved. 'There was no time for any real road test but a couple of hours on the highway convinced me that Austin is coming out with a winner, not only because this car should be quite unbeatable in its class but also because it gives you such a tremendous driving pleasure as well as confidence.' When they finally nabbed the first Austin-Cooper to arrive in California they 'found it difficult to drive without grinning from ear to ear. The performance is so startling for the overall size and appearance that it is ridiculous.' They even took the car on a weekend camping trip to the Joshua Tree National Monument, 133 miles (214km) from Los Angeles to Indio on freeways and highways, then a further 90 miles (145km) to Twenty Nine Palms on desert and often unpaved roads, before travelling the 153 miles (246km) back to Los Angeles. The Americans were amazed not only at the performance from 'the flying shoe box', but also the amount of usable interior space. 'Into the apparently minute trunk went a tent, sleeping bag, air mattress, large and crammed full pack, a large zipper handbag, a Primus stove, a gallon canteen and a pair of climbing boots.'

It was the thoroughly British *Motor* that summed up the appeal of the Cooper so succinctly, 'So much performance combined with a lot of practical merit and quite a high standard of refinement will obviously make people decide that a sum of about £600 is better spent on this model than on something bigger but no better.'

NEW 998

Modifications to the Cooper over the next two years were broadly in line with the standard car. Within six months the clumsy Se7en name was dropped. In 1963 the front brake discs were uprated while at the back aluminium suspension trumpets replaced the steel ones. The next year, 1964, was a watershed as two modifications would change the character of the car quite radically. BMC made the 998cc engine standard in January. As it was already used on the Elf and Hornet models, it made sense to introduce it to the Cooper, but in a modified form with a very different cylinder head, pistons and camshaft. It shared 1.25in SU carburettors and a three-branch exhaust system with the 997, but the camshaft and valves were different again. It had the same 0.312 lift action, but the duration was as the standard Mini (230°) as against the 252° angle of the 997. The inlet valves were larger at 1.219in (30.9mm) whereas those in the 997 were 1.156in (29.4mm). The pistons had raised crowns and compression ratios of 9:1 or 7.8:1 although very few of the low compression models were sold on the UK market.

Unlike the 997cc the new engine adopted floating small ends, which made the unit much stronger. Increasing the bore and reducing the stroke resulted in a much smoother engine, and though the maximum power at 55bhp was unchanged, it was achieved at 5,800rpm instead of 6,000rpm. The torque was also dramatically improved at 57lb.ft at 3,000rpm rather than 3,600rpm at 44lb.ft – this was a far more flexible and ultimately tougher engine.

The second key change for 1964 came in September, when Hydrolastic suspension made for a bouncier ride at speed. Many enthusiasts argued that it spoilt the Cooper. Certainly when *Motor* tested the newly suspended model they took photographic evidence to prove the change in behaviour. 'On a closed throttle the Hydrolastic suspension causes appreciable nose dive: when accelerating the car squats down at the back. Jerky driving, which emphasizes these characteristics, can make the ride uncomfortable.'

The other weakness of the 998 was its brakes, which were just not up to the job of repeatedly stopping a speeding Cooper. They were an improvement over the early models, but the S now showed it up. Part of the problem was that the S had wider, ventilated, wheel rims to accommodate bigger discs and the standard Cooper did not.

During its life the Mark I 998 Cooper was subtly updated in line with the standard model. In February 1964 the windscreen wiper arc was reduced to stop it hitting the screen rubber. By March, Dunlop SP41 radials were made standard, which significantly improved handling. In July the rear brakes had lower anti-lock pressure settings. With the advent of Hydrolastic suspension there were new gear change forks, which had a larger contact area, while the clutch was now of the diaphragm type. In October there were improved drive shaft couplings and a month later the driver's seat acquired a three-position setting. Things got a little quieter in 1965 when a radiator with 16 grilles per inch (6.3 grilles per cm) was installed, followed in May by a scroll type oil seal on the primary gears.

The 997cc Cooper was very successful. It kick-started the Cooper's rallying career and scored the model's first international victory. Sales at 25,000 were impressive, especially as the original run was meant to be just 1,000 with a weekly build of no more than twenty-five units. The 998cc version, despite getting bouncy castle Hydrolastic suspension, built on the solid foundations of the earlier car and cemented the hot little brick in buyer's affections. Most important of all were the specific Cooper developments like disc brakes and remote gear change, which would both eventually find their way onto the standard production Mini.

COOPER MARK II

The new Cooper was pure Mark II Mini with the revised grille, now made standard with a thick seven-slat design, bigger light clusters and larger rear window. The chrome trim around the door window frames was retained, but the bumper corner bars were deleted to leave the overriders behind. A major casualty of the change was the distinctively two-tone interior with black Super De Luxe trim. On the outside the same colour options were still available, increasingly though monotone schemes were becoming common.

The boot lid was now double-skinned rather than having a hardboard cover. The boot board sat on spot welded rather than riveted brackets. Mechanically, Hydrolastic was still the method of suspension and a plastic radiator fan was fitted in place of the old steel one. An all-synchromesh gearbox in 1968 was the biggest change, otherwise the Mark II car turned out to be a very short lived model, in view of the fact that the S continued in production for three more years. In terms of comparable performance its replacement was the unloved and snub-nosed 1275GT.

Cooper 998cc (1964–69) and Mark II Cooper

Engine
Type	Four cylinder in line; cast iron block transversely mounted in front
Capacity	998cc
Bore and stroke	64.6mm × 76.2mm
Output	55bhp at 5,800rpm
Compression ratio	Low compression 7.8:1
Maximum torque	57lb.ft at 3,000rpm

Transmission
Type	Front-wheel drive
Gear ratios	4-speed 3.765/5.11/7.21/12.05 13.657 (reverse) 3.44:1 (optional final drive)

Suspension
Front	Wishbones, rubber cones, Armstrong dampers; Hydrolastic from 1964
Rear	Trailing arms, rubber cones, Armstrong dampers; Hydrolastic from 1964
Steering	Rack and pinion

Brakes Hydraulic disc/drum

Tyres/Wheels 145in × 10in radial-ply/3.5in × 10in

Dimensions
Track (front)	47.75in (1,213mm)
Track (rear)	45.9in (1,166mm)
Wheelbase	80in (2,032mm)
Length	120.25in (3,054mm)
Width	55in (1,397mm)
Height	53in (1,346mm)
Unladen weight	1,400lb (635kg); Mark II Cooper 1,430lb (649kg)
Fuel capacity	5.5 gallons (25 litres)

Performance
Top speed	90mph (145kph)
Acceleration	0–60mph in 16.8 seconds
Fuel consumption	33mpg (8.5 litres per 100km)

Purchase price £679

Production 39,364

S-TYPE COOPER

Like the best performance cars, the Cooper's development became inextricably linked to competition, hence the S designation. BMC and indeed even Issigonis had been mightily impressed by the Cooper's performance on the road and in competition. Issigonis not only had the time to spare, but wanted to be involved with the Cooper this time around.

Another major influence behind the new car was BMC competitions manager Stuart Turner, who wanted a much more powerful rally weapon. He was appointed at the age of 27, just one month after the announcement of the 997 Cooper, and he set about installing professional drivers and improving workshop facilities. Turner also demanded a regular rally winning tool – the Cooper S was to be just the job.

DOWNTON POWER

Development work on the S was farmed out to consultants like Daniel Richmond of Downton Engineering. Richmond's tweaked 997 Cooper was studied closely at Longbridge before the final decision was made in the winter of 1962 to build an S model in a quantity of 1,000 units to qualify for Group 2 competition. Despite the involvement of outsiders, control of the project was down to Issigonis. It was decided to concentrate on an 1,100cc in the interests of competition, giving BMC the option of stroking the unit up or down depending on the class they were considering.

The resulting over-square 1,071cc engine kept to this brief and the unit itself was very different from a standard A series. Under the bonnet it was easy to spot the new head, which had an extra holding-down stud and twin 1.25in (32mm) SU carburettors. The block had also changed because the tappet side covers, familiar sights on an 848cc, were missing as the outer cylinder bores were moved further apart while the inner two got closer. The engine internals were heavily revised; in particular the crankshaft was made from special EN40B steel and nitrided to make it harder. The valve guides also received a similar treatment, being constructed from Nimonic 80, while the valves themselves had stellite faces welded on to make them harder wearing.

Although capable of revving right up to 7,200rpm, the power of 70bhp was delivered at 6,200rpm. To handle this the standard Cooper gearbox was fitted, with optional lower final drive ratio and a close ratio gearbox. Stopping it all were thicker (0.375in) and larger diameter (7.5in) discs with servo assistance, plus a tweaked rear brake pressure-limiting valve. Ventilated steel wheels helped keep the brakes cool and these were now 4.5in wide (rather than 3.5in on the standard Cooper) with just the standard hub caps. Higher ratio steering – lock to lock was 2.3 turns – also made the S an even more manageable performance car.

S specification was identical to the Cooper, apart from those all-important distinguishing badges on the bonnet and boot lid. Inside, the upholstery was equally Super De Luxe; the speedometer was calibrated up to 120mph (193kph).

S TESTS

Magazine road testers all responded well to the improved performance of the S, its superior braking and Dunlop SP Sport tyres. One penalty was increased fuel consumption, although the optional right hand tank would double the capacity to 11 gallons (50 litres). First, *Autocar* squeezed a 13.5 second 0–60mph time, a 91mph (146kph) top

Cooper S 1,071cc (1963–65); 970cc (1964–65)

Engine
Type	Four cylinder in line; cast iron block transversely mounted in front
Capacity	1,071/970cc
Bore and stroke	70.64mm × 68.26mm/70.6mm × 61.91mm
Output	70bhp at 6,200rpm/65bhp at 6,500rpm
Compression ratio	9:1/10:1
Maximum torque	62lb.ft at 4,500rpm/57lb.ft at 5,000rpm

Transmission
Type	Front-wheel drive
Gear ratios	4-speed 3.765/5.11/7.21/12.04 13.657 (reverse) 3.44:1 (optional final drive) optional close ratio

Suspension
Front	Wishbones, rubber cones, Armstrong dampers; Hydrolastic from 1964
Rear	Trailing arms, rubber cones, Armstrong dampers; Hydrolastic from 1964
Steering	Rack and pinion

Brakes   Servo-assisted disc/drum

Tyres/Wheels   145in × 10in radial-ply/3.5in (4.5in) × 10in

Dimensions
Track (front)	48.4in (1,229mm)
Track (rear)	46.9in (1,191mm)
Wheelbase	80in (2,032mm)
Length	120.25in (3,054mm)
Width	55in (1,397mm)
Height	53in (1,346mm)
Unladen weight	1,410lb (640kg)
Fuel capacity	5.5 gallons (25 litres)

Performance
Top speed	90mph (145kph)/89mph (143kph)
Acceleration	0–60mph in 13.5/11.8 seconds
Fuel consumption	29mpg (9.7 litres per 100km)/30mpg (9.4 litres per 100km)

Purchase price   £695

Production
1,071	4,031
970	963

speed and a 19.2 second time for the standing quarter mile (0.4km). Two weeks later *Motor* managed the 0–60mph in 12.9 seconds, a 94.5mph (152.1kph) top speed and the standing quarter in 18.9 seconds. They also raved about the brakes. 'The braking powers of the S are formidable and in complete harmony with its performance. The disc-front, drum-rear, combination, allied to Hydrovac servo assistance gives extremely effective braking with only gentle pedal pressure, while repeated use brought no evidence of brake fade.' They summed it up very nicely when they concluded, 'In all the Mini-Cooper S is a car of delightful Jekyll and Hyde character, with astonishing performance concealed within its unpretentious Mini skin.'

By the time that Bill Boddy got his hands on the 1071S for *Motor Sport* he had pushed the 0–60mph time down to 11.9 seconds and 18.7 for the standing quarter although top speed was only 92mph (148kph). He found the S slightly docile, an 'Excellent balance between good acceleration and civilized step-off, between ultra powerful brakes and sensitive, wet-road retardation.' However, he did find the almost luxury interior, flecked upholstery and trim incongruous in a rally car.

The Americans were suitably impressed with their $2,500 version of the 1071S in *Auto*. 'A belt in the back and a few seconds later I glanced at the tach … and then looked at the speedometer. It was swinging rapidly towards 90mph and we were still in third!' They managed to get pulled over by the Highway Patrol, who could barely believe that something so small could go so fast. They had a debate about speedometer accuracy and the police followed for a few miles and confirmed that the Mini really was exceeding the speed limit by a massive margin. The police were equally impressed and never even issued a speeding ticket.

Ultimately though, 'It is in the areas of ride, handling and manoeuvrability that the Austin-Cooper S is truly outstanding.' Typically they found the specification on the basic side: 'While we could make some snide remarks about the mirror, wipers and interior light, few creature comforts have been sacrificed for size and performance.' Their sum-up was a ringing endorsement. 'Not many cars come down the pike which are all sweetness and light. The Austin-Cooper S is one of them. Sure … it's an ugly little pumpkin. It has some minor faults which should be corrected. But in spite of all this we can't imagine a sports car we would rather have. Nor can we remember a car we enjoyed more in the testing.'

The production run for the first S had been set at 1,000, but that number had been exceeded fourfold when it was discontinued in March 1964. But then, as had been planned, the long and short stroke versions of this engine were launched within months of each other.

970S

The short stroke and short-lived 970S model was in fact introduced after the 1275S. The nine month production run was purely to special order and homologation specific as just under 1,000 were built to qualify for the 1,000cc class and International Group 2 Touring Car Championship. However, its influence extended into the late 1960s when it was still used by the factory to snatch a class win in certain events; Tony Fall won the 1966 Polish Rally in a 970S. Its forte was saloon car racing, where highly tuned variants dominated the sport.

This was not a cheap engine to build, although its effects were widely appreciated. Despite producing just 65bhp at 6,500rpm, it was almost as quick as the

1275S. The 970 was a smooth, high revving unit, but obviously not as flexible as the larger S, which produced a useful 79lb.ft at 3,000rpm against the 970's 55lb.ft at 3,500rpm. Like the rest of the range it was uprated to run on Hydrolastic suspension after just three months production. A few months later, the 970S had done its job and was discontinued.

1275S

The Cooper S became synonymous with the 1,275cc unit. It produced a useful 76bhp that was not only torquey but flexible and reliable. This engine would go on to outlive all the other A series engines and keep the Mini running well into the 1990s. Getting it built in the first place was not easy, as George Harriman had trouble believing that that the original 850cc engine could be stretched to that capacity. In the end he trusted John Cooper's judgement and told the development team to get on with it. The result was probably the most remarkable Cooper of all. If the original 997 had been a

revelation this new S reached the magic 100mph (160kph) and almost halved the Cooper's 0–60mph time. It was clearly from another planet in terms of performance.

1275 MEETS THE PRESS

The first versions of the 1275S that reached the press test fleets had dry suspension. It was John Bolster for *Autosport* who managed some astonishingly quick performance figures, getting the 0–60mph time down to 9 seconds, the quarter mile (0.4km) in 17.6 seconds and a top speed of 100mph (160kph). 'Up to 60 or 70 mph the acceleration is tremendous ... it cannot be too strongly emphasized that this model bears no resemblance to the typical modified Mini, many of which are rough and noisy to an extent which becomes wearisome for everyday motoring.'

Autocar were not successful in achieving such impressive performance times and unlike Bolster found the car a little rough on occasions. 'Top-end roughness could be felt as quite a violent vibration through the gear lever ... There is another vibration,

Under the bonnet of the 1275S, the engine that would not only power the Cooper into the 1970s, but also take the Mini into the 1990s in catalysed and injected form.

corresponding with the idling speed just below 1,000rpm, which causes the steering column to shake, and the wiper blades to flutter on the windscreen.' However the magazine concluded, 'In almost any degree of traffic, country roads, trunk routes, or city streets, the 1275S is one of the quickest ways of getting from A to B in safety. Far from a quart squeezed into the proverbial pint pot, this car has handling and braking well within its high standards of performance.'

Motor also had a few reservations when the same test car started to sup oil at 75 miles per pint (210km per litre) and it proved to be a touch slower than tuning company specials, although they still thought it a remarkable car. 'Even if some of the novelty has worn off, our enthusiasm for Mini motoring reached new peaks after only 1,500 miles in this car. With a maximum speed of 96.8mph, vivid acceleration and still further improved handling, it is enormous fun to drive and just about the most practical toy that £750 will buy. It has most of the failings of other Minis – uncomfortable seats, an awkward driving position, bumpy ride – plus some of its own like very heavy oil consumption, but the sheer delight of driving was adequate compensation for us.'

1275 SPECIFICATION

The trim specification of the 1275 was identical to the 1071 and 970 models, although a laminated windscreen was standard. Likewise, model developments were largely in line with the ordinary Minis. So of course Hydrolastic suspension was added in 1964, but not to all-round approval. Henry Manney took a Hydrolastic S for a spin on the Goodwood race circuit for *Road and Track* in 1965. 'The increased suspension movement necessary for carrying Auntie Dollie and her parcels does not seem to agree with it at speed. There was more lean and the customary Mini on rails feeling was slightly lessened, even if you could stuff it through tight corners on full understeer as before.'

By contrast devout Mini fan John Bolster thoroughly approved of the new system. 'On the road, the Hydrolastic Mini feels almost soggy at parking speeds, but the suspension seems to become progressively harder as the velocity increases. The improvement in riding comfort is very great … For use on the road, though I am completely sold on it, from every point of view.'

Motor were sceptical about the Hydrolastic suspension, which 'improved the ride – mainly by converting pitch into bounce – but it also gives the impression that there is a good deal more roll than occurred in earlier Minis.' Some of these criticisms were addressed with an improved system from 1966. These were higher rate units with a steel and rubber lower wishbone bush, strengthened suspension mountings and a flange to fix solid universal joints onto the driveshaft. Other significant changes were an oil cooler and twin fuel tanks in 1966.

Many road testers had commented on the fact that the S seemed to burn a lot of oil and would benefit from the addition of a cooler to reduce consumption. Fuel consumption was the other worry as a hard driven S might struggle to do 150 miles (241km) on a tiny 5.5 gallon (25 litre) tank. However, a second (right-hand) tank had been an option for some time, sensibly doubling the range and balancing the dramatic rear profile. Significant options included reclining seats in 1965 and a heated rear window a year later.

COOPER S MARK II

The Cooper S entered its second phase in line with other more mundane models and ended up looking just as standard because a

Cooper S 1,275cc (Mark I, II and III)

Engine

Type	Four cylinder in line; cast iron block transversely mounted in front
Capacity	1,275cc
Bore and stroke	70.6mm × 81.33mm
Output	76bhp at 5,800rpm
Compression ratio	9.75:1
Maximum torque	62lb.ft at 4,500rpm/57lb.ft at 5,000rpm

Transmission

Type	Front-wheel drive
Gear ratios	4-speed 3.765/5.11/7.21/12.04 13.657 (reverse) 3.44:1 (optional final drive) optional close ratio

Suspension

Front	Wishbones, rubber cones, Armstrong dampers; Hydrolastic from 1964
Rear	Trailing arms, rubber cones, Armstrong dampers; Hydrolastic from 1964
Steering	Rack and pinion

Brakes   Servo-assisted disc/drum

Tyres/Wheels   145in × 10in radial-ply/3.5in(4.5in) × 10in

Dimensions

Track (front)	47.53in (1,207mm)
Track (rear)	46.31in (1,176mm)
Wheelbase	80in (2,032mm)
Length	120.25in (3,054mm)
Width	55in (1,397mm)
Height	53in (1,346mm)
Unladen weight	1,535lb (696kg); Mark III 1,525lb (692kg)
Luggage capacity	4cu ft (113 litres) from 1966
Fuel capacity	5.5 gallons (25 litres); 11 gallons (50 litres) from 1966

Performance

Top speed	96mph (154kph)
Acceleration	0–60mph in 11.2 seconds
Fuel consumption	29mpg (9.7 litres per 100km)

Purchase price

1964	£695
1967	£849
1970	£942

Production

Mark I	14,313
Mark II	6,329
Mark III	19,511

Mark II Cooper S. A larger rear window and light clusters were the main changes for 1967.

An Austin Mini Cooper in Mark II guise. This was the last official Cooper for twenty years.

contrasting roof colour became less common. Inside, Super De Luxe trim took the place of the more flamboyant two-tone variety. A new Mark II 1275 badge and either a new oval Morris (white background), or Austin (black background) S badge at the front helped distinguish the S, while 4.5in rims also set the car apart. An all-synchromesh gearbox in 1968 was the only significant update.

COOPER S MARK III

Announced in November 1969, the Mark III S was the sole surviving Cooper representative to take the great name into the 1970s. The production of separate Austin and Morris variants continued until March 1970 but then the generic Mini marque took over as the Cooper S entered its final, Mark III phase. If enthusiasts thought that the Mark II was indistinguishable from a standard 1000 model, this latest model became completely anonymous. The grille was the same, as was the corporate 'Mini' bonnet badge, while the door trim and seats were shared with the Clubman. Blink and you could miss the oblong badge on the boot, which still bore the legend 'Mini Cooper S'. What the Cooper did retain from the old model was the Hydrolastic suspension. Although the rest of the range (except the Clubman) had switched back to the dry rubber cone system, the surplus Hydrolastic sub-frames were foisted back onto the Cooper.

This is where part one of the Cooper connection ends. Donald Stokes had taken over the reins at BMC as it became BL. There was never any official agreement between Cooper and BMC about developing the Coopers, just a straight £2 royalty on each unit sold. When Stokes came along that nominal sum was regarded as extravagant and Cooper's involvement unnecessary in the new BL scheme of things – despite the fact that Cooper and its unprecedented sequence of sporting success had paid off handsomely in terms of sales, international publicity and prestige.

The Cooper could not really be replaced and BL did not really try. The 1275GT and

Mark III Cooper S.

1300GT were marketing exercises rather than serious attempts to develop the small sporting car, and the same could be said of the future Cooper. At least the Cooper concept was not quite dead, only resting and waiting for a Far Eastern revival.

COOPERS RE-BODIED

If any car lent itself to being reinvented, re-bodied and reinvigorated it had to be the Mini, which more often than not turned out to be a Cooper. That neat drivetrain package gave any engineer and designer plenty of positioning options. Not only that, the A series engine was infinitely tuneable. The results on a good day could be brilliant. Quite often though they were regrettable and down-right doggish. Here is a selection of the best and most famous made-over Mini Coopers.

MINI SPRINT

We have all seen Minis with a roof that looks like it has been used as a skateboard by an elephant, but very few of these are the genuine article. The story goes back to *Cars and Car Conversions*, the monthly bible of the inveterate club racer and go faster freak, when contributor Clive Trickey demonstrated that it could be done. The design passed through several hands, at one point being called the Walker GT3 before coachbuilders Stewart and Arden called it the Mini Sprint in 1967.

Cooper S Minis were stripped, the roof pillars were increased in rake and reduced by 1.5in (38mm) and a similar amount was removed from the middle of the car. Then all the external seams were removed for a smoother look and 40sq in (258sq cm) less of aerodynamic resistance. The wings were reshaped and rectangular headlights fitted.

(Above) *Line-up of Coopers. Standard Cooper in the centre flanked by two Mini Sprints.*

(Opposite) *ADO 34 was a serious and fascinating proposal for an MG Midget based on Cooper S running gear. This pretty car was styled and built by Pininfarina.*

The driver sat a little more comfortably because the seat frames were lowered and reclined.

BROADSPEED GT

Tuning genius and respected Mini racer Ralph Broad came up with a fast-backed Mini and put in on sale in 1966. With lowered Hydrolastic suspension, fine engineering and structurally sound roof conversion, it really looked like a scaled down Aston Martin.

Five versions were offered, a basic 850cc at £808, a GT based on the Cooper at £915 and a 1275 Cooper S badged as a GT De Luxe for £1,068. This had reclining seats, a folding rear seat for extra luggage, pile carpets, a comprehensive fascia and plastic bumpers with rubber and chrome inserts. Not only that, a Super de Luxe was offered with a more highly tuned Broadspeed Stage III engine (100bhp) and a full race GTS version to special order. Only twenty-eight were built, many ending up in Spain.

COOPER VIP

John Cooper sent a Mini Cooper to Nuccino Bertone in 1966 and got a thoroughly revised one back – a cleaner re-style with a new grille, larger indicators and Riley Elf bumpers. Inside, it had lots of leather, reshaped front seats, head restraints, a lowered steering column, revised dashboard and electric windows. When production did not happen, Cooper customers were offered these updates at a price, but few were built.

RADFORD COOPERS

Of all the coachbuilders and specialists involved with Minis in the 1960s, Radford was perhaps the most successful and innovative. Inspired by the work of Hoopers, who had conjured up an eye-catching wicker-worked special for Peter Sellers, they made their own version. Harold Radford, who was used to installing cocktail cabinets in Rolls Royce limousines, did much the same with

Mini de Ville – an overweight miniature limousine from 1963.

(Above) *Hatchback by Radford, originally built for Peter Sellers and even copied by BMC, who built a one-off for Transport Minister Earnest Marples (right).*

their first effort in 1963, producing the Cooper Mini de Ville Grande Luxe. It was described as 'the chauffeur driven Mini' and featured redesigned white leather seats, an instrument binnacle in front of the driver, two-tone silver over charcoal Rolls Royce paint, electric windows, Webasto sunroof, stereo radio and lambswool carpets.

Radford still producing a mini Mercedes out of a Mini Cooper S, sometime in 1971.

It cost £1,100 and with the extra weight of all the gadgets was disappointingly slow. Radford never made that mistake again; he used Downton tuned engines to make up the shortfall and leave a standard Cooper for dead.

OGLE MINI

Industrial Designer David Ogle had underground trains and helicopters to his credit when he turned his attention to building and marketing a small sports car. First revealed in 1962 with a 997cc Cooper engine, the bodywork was made from GRP (Glass Reinforced Plastic), which enclosed the Mini's floor pan, which was also reinforced. Badged as the SX1000 it flopped in America, the market it was intended for, but sold steadily in the UK as the Lightweight GT and Mini 850 GT. Just

sixty-six examples were built, but after Ogle's untimely death the manufacturing rights were sold.

The Fletcher GT, with its ugly new nose, was equally unprofitable. Just four were sold.

CRAYFORD MINI COOPER SPRINT

Legendary coachbuilders Crayford opened up almost every significant car built in the 1960s. Among the many attempts to build a fresh-air Mini theirs was the best, and was announced in September 1963. Any Mini could be converted for £129. They installed floor section box members, door pillar and scuttle reinforcement with transverse stiffening and waist level stiffeners. The side screens could be retained for the sliding windows, but there were also removable versions.

Crayford convertible.

UNIPOWER

Universal Power Drives built forestry tractors. In 1968 they constructed what is probably the best mid-engined Mini sports car ever. Originally built by Andrew Hedges with an aluminium body for racing driver Roy Pierpoint, UPD bought the rights and entered production.

At £1,200 (prior to the required Mini or Cooper engine being fitted) it was not cheap. It had a sophisticated tubular steel chassis, GRP body and the suspension was all independent with coil springs. With 998cc power it could get to 100mph (160kph), but with 1,275cc on board 120mph (193kph) was well within its grasp.

Best of all the mini-based specials, the Unipower GT. Mid-engined and a poor man's Lotus Europa.

MINI MARCOS

The only British car to finish the 1966 Le Mans was a Marcos. Launched just a year earlier by the company that bore Jem Marsh and Frank Costin's names, the Mini Marcos was not a pretty sight, but it was tremendously successful on the track and as a commercial product. It had a complicated parentage, based on a Paul Emery designed prototype, with a Mini Van floor pan and built by Marcos's parent company Falcon for amateur racer Dizzy Addicot.

It was hurriedly prepared for production, hence the oddly styled monocoque body. Mini sub-frames were bolted on through metal plates with wooden floor reinforcement. From the same gene pool sprang the MINIJEM, which was almost identical and had competition success, with sales that topped 350.

The Marcos had a chequered history, got a tailgate in 1971, and after the bankruptcy of Marcos passed through a variety of owners. Marsh re-launched the Marcos Mark V in 1991 as a result of a huge order from Japan. The MINIJEM had an equally unfortunate career and went out of production in 1976 when the UK kit car industry collapsed. It was later revived in the early 1980s as the Kingfisher.

1960s MINI TUNERS

A class apart from the rest was Downton Engineering. Proprietor and expert tuner Daniel Richmond had official endorsement from BMC and was in close contact with all those involved with the Mini: Issigonis, Moulton, Cooper, competition boss Turner and company boss Harriman. From his base in Downton, Wiltshire, Richmond began tinkering with the Mini in 1959 and the results were always incredible. As well as official projects for BMC, which included work on the Cooper and the cylinder head on Group 2 1275s that was never bettered, Richmond had a roster of eager clients.

After Radford had finished adorning Coopers, Richmond would put the performance back plus a little more. Steve McQueen, racing driver Dan Gurney and the legendary Enzo Ferrari all owned Minis that passed through his spotless workshops. Richmond claimed that he achieved his remarkable results by attention to detail.

The Mini Marcos.

The company proved to be a finishing school for many A series exponents including racer Gordon Spice, Jan Odor (who went on to found Janspeed) and Richard Longman.

An equally evocative name from the 1960s was Broadspeed. Best known for running a team of highly competitive Coopers, they would also prepare cars for private customers. *Car and Car Conversions* took a 1275 for a spin in January 1966: 'The chief weaknesses of the Cooper S are noise, vibration and ... an excessive oil consumption. The car we have been testing is quieter, suffers from practically no vibration, despite its ability to survive a 2,000rpm increase in engine speed ... This car did 113mph in one direction, and will get to sixty, two up, in under nine seconds.' That conversion cost £100 and comprised a modified cylinder head (with larger inlet valves, ports and tracts), polished ports, re-contoured combustion chambers a compression ratio of 10.5:1, modified inlet manifold, 1.5in SU H4 carburettors, a road/race camshaft and modified exhaust manifold.

Among the many hundreds of companies that made Minis go faster was Yimkin Engineering based in central London. To tweak the basic Minor and Seven they simply used a modified cylinder head and special needle for the SU carburettor. With a raised compression ratio of 8.8:1 the performance improvements were slight: they added just 5mph (8kph) to the top speed and knocked only 0.5 seconds off the 0–60mph time. The car was made famous for being motor racing legend Juan Manuel Fangio's introduction to Mini motoring.

Arden Racing from Solihull were quick off the mark with a modified 850cc. A modified cylinder head, revised inlet and exhaust manifold, additional 1.25in SU carburettor and new exhaust silencer were part of the package, as was an optional electronic rev counter. The top speed went up to 85mph (137kph) and the 0–60mph time to 20 seconds.

Nerus Engineering had a racing background in Formula 2 and produced budget kits to transform 850s into Coopers and Coopers into S types. There were Stage 1 heads. Stage 2 heads, cams and exhaust systems and a Stage 3 package for competition work. Up to 83bhp was on offer.

Alexander Engineering from Buckinghamshire offered conversions for the Cooper, including a big bore model displacing

The cockpit of a Radford styled, Downton tuned Cooper S.

Car Magazine *put a Downton-tuned Radford Cooper S through its paces.*

1,122cc with forged pistons, new big end bearings, a new camshaft, re-ported cylinder and twin 1.5in SU carburettors mounted on a modified inlet and exhaust manifold. The improvement over the standard 997cc Cooper was dramatic, as the car could top 100mph (160kph) and do 0–60mph in just 10 seconds.

Taurus Performance Tuning, another A series specialist, tickled Minis and Coopers with larger H4 SU carburettors, a skimmed and reworked cylinder head and a hotter camshaft. With their revised exhaust and Koni adjustable suspension this was a potent package, teasing 100bhp from a 1,275cc Cooper.

When it came to tuning equipment, Speedwell produced a large range of A series compatible parts. They also built some radical road cars, the most notable being the Courier, which was based on the Mini Estate. The 850cc engine was enlarged to 1,152cc; with a special crankshaft, flowed cylinder, performance camshaft and H4 carburettors it all added up to 91bhp at 6,600rpm. Lowered suspension and Girling servo assistance with anti-fade brake lining meant that the 100mph (160kph) estate could handle and stop safely.

The many other Mini tuners included such famous names as Oselli and Janspeed, who are still in business today.

12 Resurrection Shuffle

*'It's got quite a bit of the old S about it ... gets the
old adrenalin going, if you know what I mean ...'*

John Cooper

Despite reports to the contrary, the Mini Cooper did not die in 1971. From his British Leyland franchise John Cooper could still sell you a brand new Mini until the mid-1980s, when he switched allegiance to Honda. Cooper had built a 1,071cc model in 1975 featuring the traditional Cooper colour scheme, so the genuine Mini Cooper never really went away.

Always thinking ahead, John Cooper Garages developed the Metro Monaco in 1982, taking the new hatchback in 1.3 HLS trim and tuning it for 100mph (160kph) performance. On the outside were Wolfrace alloy wheels, a bold Cooper logo and stripes from sill to waist height. It predated the introduction of the dire MG versions, but BL were reluctant to cover the car under their warranty so the project did not progress any further. But there were stirrings in the Far East.

BIG IN JAPAN

John Cooper had been selling performance conversion kits to Japan for some time and the President of Austin Rover of Japan was well aware of the interest in the cars. To boost demand he contacted Cooper and

asked if an MG Metro engine could be put into a Mini. Cooper obliged by doing so with a Mayfair: the Japanese loved it. A formal request was made to initiate production of 1,000 units, but getting the model through type approval put senior management off the idea. Instead, Cooper satisfied the demand for a go-faster Far Eastern Mini by putting together a kit in a timber packing case that fitted into a rear seat.

In 1989, management changes at Rover coincided with the Mini's 30th anniversary. They liked the conversion and asked for a couple of cars to be produced so that a warranty test could be carried out. After 20,000 miles, approval was granted and the company listened to John Cooper's suggestion for a celebratory model. Production of a Cooper look-alike in the shape of the special edition Racing and Flames, which had duo tone paintwork and Miniliteish alloy wheels, was the result. Just in case anyone was in any doubt of their future intentions a John Cooper Conversion Kit was added to the options list. This comprised twin SU HS2 carburettors, a polished and flowed Janspeed cylinder head, bigger inlet valves, hardened valve inserts and a 9.75:1 compression ratio. A twin box exhaust system and 3.1:1 final drive completed the

A Cooper for the 1990s in full retro effect. The winged bonnet badge is a mix of the original Morris and Austin Cooper items. It has Minilite type wheels, themselves copies of Cooper Formula. This is the production model, without the extra driving lights and the limited edition white bonnet stripes with John Cooper's signature on them.

performance picture. The output was boosted to 64bhp at 6,000rpm and the 998cc engine became less of an also-ran.

LIMITED EDITION

The full scale resurrection of the Cooper occurred in 1990, when Rover again listened to John Cooper's wisdom and agreed to fit the 1,275cc engine to the car. He built a twin carburettor prototype that went down very well with senior management, but the twin carburettors presented a type approval problem. In the end, the sub-frame had to be moved 0.375in (10mm) forward. All was then clear for Rover to take the Mini Thirty body shell and combine it with a 61bhp, single carburettor, catalyst equipped 1,275cc engine last seen in the old MG Metro. In

performance terms, it was nowhere near the old Cooper S, with an 87mph (140kph) 0–60mph time and a top speed of 12.2 seconds, but it was a move in the right direction.

At first it appeared in a limited edition of 1,650 cars featuring white bonnet stripes. Minilite type alloy wheels, glass sunroof, driving lamps and door mirrors were all standard. Chrome also made a comeback with a slatted grille, bumpers and a winged Cooper bonnet badge. The two-tone colour schemes were back: white roofs were contrasted by green, black, or red bodywork. The famous Cooper laurel logo decorated the rear side panel and a side stripe led to the tip of the front wing. On the inside there was half leather seat trim, a red carpet and a red steering wheel. The first 1,000 for the UK market came complete with John Cooper's signature on the bonnet stripe.

170

WELCOMED BACK

By September 1990 the Cooper became a proper production model. In the interests of economy the bonnet stripes, sunroof and spotlamps were dumped, though they could be ordered as extras. Inside, the upholstery turned to cloth and the steering wheel went back to black, as did the carpets.

Car Magazine in their September 1990 issue undertook a monumental comparison, pitting the new Cooper against the ten best hot hatch rivals of the time. The line up was impressive: Mini Cooper, Alfa Romeo 33 16V, Citroën AX GT, Fiat Uno Turbo, Ford Fiesta RS Turbo, Mazda 323F GT, Metro GTi 16V, Peugeot 205 GTi 1.6, Renault 5GT Turbo, Vauxhall Astra GTE 16V and Volkswagen Golf GTi. Editor Gavin Green placed the car first, 'There's no doubt, on the Yorkshire assault course chosen for our shoot-out, it was the most inept. It groaned and whined when the others kept quiet; it bucked and bolted when the others gently cantered; and the seats are plain uncomfortable,

seriously deficient in lateral support and rear seat movement. But I loved it … I suppose I loved it because I've always loved Minis. I also like small cars – any small car – and after more than 30 years, no-one has invented a smaller one.'

L.J.K. Setright also voted the Cooper in at number one, 'The Mini shows that they are all too big, all slaves to showroom fashion. None shows the staunch independence that makes the Mini as refreshing as it always was, and makes it impossible for the others to bear comparison with it.'

RETURN OF THE S

In March 1991 the Cooper got much nearer to the original car's sparkle with another conversion kit that finally turned it into an S. The oil-cooled engine now produced 78bhp and a handling package included specially developed low profile Dunlop SP Sport 165/60 R12 tyres and adjustable shock absorbers.

Inside the Cooper. This is the cockpit of a 1991 1.3i – not much different from the standard Mayfair.

Performance Car tested the fully equipped S in July 1991. The base car was a £6,947 Rover Mini Cooper, the engine S pack added £1,878 and the Sports Handling Pack a further £671. 'The bottom line is power up from 61 to 78bhp and torque up 67 to 78lb.ft, these achieved at 6,000 and 3,250rpm respectively. What it means on the road is 0–60 mph in a little over 10 seconds – quicker off the mark than the Vauxhall Nova SR or the VW Polo GT and a top speed close on 100mph. Power and performance figures that match almost exactly those of the original car. Fuel economy remains outstanding; we averaged 36mpg and we weren't hanging about.' They really enjoyed driving it. 'Few cars can match the Cooper S for sheer grip; those that can tend to be called Quattro or Cosworth … Those chunky Dunlops really bite and when they finally release their grip the S drifts through bends with astonishing poise, steering on the throttle. The tighter the turn the more the Cooper simply gets stuck in, sometimes lifting an inside wheel but never raising a doubt.' Finally John Cooper himself rang up to ask how they were getting along with the car, 'I didn't want the stripes on the bonnet, but otherwise it's got quite a bit of the old S about it. And it certainly handles. It gets the old adrenalin going, if you know what I mean … '

INJECTED COOPER

By October 1991 the Cooper was modified to comply with emissions legislation as carburettors were replaced by fuel injection and a three-way catalytic converter. The new Cooper 1.3i was usefully quicker than the old model, producing 63bhp at 5,700rpm and doing 60mph in 11.5 seconds, with a maximum of 92mph (148kph). The 1.3i came with those distinctive white bonnet stripes as standard once more. Inside, there were lightning pattern seat facings with leather bolsters and red piping. The red leather steering wheel was back along with equally bright carpets and even red instrument needles. In-car entertainment was uprated with an R652 system nudging the passenger's knees.

Enthusiasts did not have to wait long for the 1.3i to get the full S treatment. A factory warranted conversion turned the car into the Si, which made the Cooper something special again with a 0–60mph time of 10 seconds and a 100mph (160kph) top speed.

In March 1993 the emphasis was on beating the thieves who had turned the Cooper into the wrong kind of 'hot' car. Visible vehicle identification numbers were etched onto the front and rear screens, and an alarm and engine immobilizer were added. An internal bonnet release was finally made standard, along with a passenger door mirror. The seats were modified, as were the door bins.

Special editions started to afflict the Cooper in 1991, although Rover cunningly disguised them as add-on, packs and kits. First, there was the Italian Job pack, which amounted to spotlamps, bonnet stripes and moulded boot liner. An RAC pack added tinted glass, a sunroof and mud flaps; the finishing touches included a sump guard, locking wheel nuts and a fire extinguisher.

A Monte Carlo Anniversary pack in 1994 was largely cosmetic apart from a pair of spotlamps, and included white racing squares on the doors, decals and a coachline. *Car Magazine* included this model in its September 1994 assessment of the 'Cheap Champs' and picked five cars that dished up budget-priced fun by the bucketful. Gavin Green reckoned, 'You don't have to go fast to have fun. Interesting cars aren't always good cars. It's possible to be kicked in the bum, get your eardrums bashed, be cramped, feel like you're riding inside a salt shaker – and still

Mini Cooper 1.3i in full flight ...

... And this is the injected unit powering it.

Mini Cooper/1.3i (July 1990 to October 1996)

Engine

Type	Four cylinder in line; cast iron block transversely mounted in front
Capacity	1,275cc
Bore and stroke	70.64 × 81.33mm
Output	61bhp at 5,550rpm/63bhp at 5,700rpm
Compression ratio	10.5:1/10.0:1
Maximum torque	61lb.ft at 3,000rpm/70lb.ft at 3,900rpm

Transmission

Type	Front-wheel drive
Gear ratios	4-speed 3.11/4.43/6.79/11.34 (reverse) 11.40
	4-speed automatic 3.76/5.49/6.94/10.11

Suspension

Front	Independent, wishbones with rubber cones and telescopic dampers
Rear	Independent trailing arms with rubber cones and telescopic dampers
Steering	Rack and pinion

Brakes Disc/drum

Tyres/Wheels 165/60 R12/145/70 radial ply 12 × 4.5in steel

Dimensions

Track (front)	49.2in (1,250mm)
Track (rear)	47.4in (1,204mm)
Wheelbase	80.1in (2,035mm)
Length	120.25in (3,054mm)
Width	55.5in (1,410mm)
Height	53.25 (1,353mm)
Unladen weight	1,530lb (694kg)
Luggage capacity	4.1cu ft (116 litres)
Fuel capacity	7.5 gallons (34 litres)

Performance

Top speed	87mph (140kph)/92mph (148kph)
Acceleration	0–60mph in 12/11.5 seconds
Fuel consumption	37.3mpg (94.2 litres per 100km)/36.6mpg (47.1 litres per 100km)

Purchase price £6,595/£7,845

have a great time. I know this because I have just driven a Mini again … You wear a Mini, like a track suit, a pair of jeans or a suit (and the Mini is one of the few cars that can carry off all three roles). Never mind that the Mini isn't great transport, not by state of the art sensible (boring) 1990s standards. Instead, it's a little motorized chum.'

In 1996 it was the Cooper's turn to celebrate 35 years in production, hence the Mini Cooper 35. Based on the standard Cooper 1.3i, its paint scheme was pure 1960s featuring Almond Green bodywork with a contrasting white roof, just as the original Cooper was presented in 1961. There were also gunmetal-finish alloy wheels fitted with 165/60 R12 tyres, 'Cooper' wheel centre badges, body-coloured wheel arch extensions and door mirrors. There were two fog lamps in addition to the standard main beam auxiliary lamps. On the inside the seats were inspired by the two-tone originals with Porcelain Green leather upholstery, incorporating a Cooper logo embossed into the seats' back; with colour co-ordinated

leather steering wheel and gear knob. The Mini Cooper 35 retailed for £8,195 and only 200 were built for the British market.

The Mini Cooper can be viewed as little more than a slick marketing exercise. Certainly Rowan Atkinson, writing about it in the November 1991 issue of *Car Magazine*, was not convinced. After laying into the limited editions that multiplied during the 1980s, Atkinson turned his attentions to the Cooper. 'The depths of tackiness plumbed are still evident on the new Cooper. The nostalgia bred white stripes, white roof, tacky unpainted flared wheel arches, and driving lamps, just tinsel fripperies that attempt to distract you from the fact that they have not spent any money at all. The only attractive Cooper element in my book is the stainless rather than black look radiator grille, which merely redresses an improvement of a few years back. The original Mini shape is so good, so neat, that anyone who considers these nostalgia add-ons an improvement must be barmy. The car looks like a mobile Halfords promotion.'

Mini Cooper 35th Anniversary, seen here in the hands of 1968 European Touring Car Champion John Rhodes who is negotiating the chicane at the Goodwood race track. The car was finished in Almond Green and White paintwork, just like the first Coopers.

Mini and Cooper (from October 1996)

Engine
Type	Four cylinder in line; cast iron block transversely mounted in front
Capacity	1,275cc
Bore and stroke	70.64 × 81.33mm
Output	63PS/46kW at 5,500rpm
Compression ratio	10.5:1
Maximum torque	95Nm at 3,000rpm

Transmission
Type	Front-wheel drive
Gear ratios	4-speed 5.7/9.6/14.7/21.0

Suspension
Front	Independent, wishbones with rubber cones and telescopic dampers
Rear	Independent trailing arms with rubber cones and telescopic dampers
Steering	Rack and pinion

Brakes   Disc/drum

Tyres/Wheels   145/70 R12 radial ply; 12 and 13in

Dimensions
Track (front)	48.8in (1,240mm)
Track (rear)	47.6in (1,209mm)
Wheelbase	80.1in (2,035mm)
Length	120.25in (3,054mm)
Width	55.5in (1,410mm)
Height	53.25in (1,353mm)
Unladen weight	1,576 to 1,587lb (715 to 720kg)
Luggage capacity	4.1cu ft (116 litres)
Fuel capacity	7.5 gallons (34 litres)

Performance
Top speed	90mph (145kph)
Acceleration	0–60mph in 12.2 seconds
Fuel consumption combined	43mpg (6.5 litres per 100km)

Purchase price   £8,995

Cooper S, still going strong in 1996. John Cooper stands next to Rover's standard 1996 specification Cooper, and his son Michael leans on a John Cooper Garages 'Mini Cooper S' as Rover insisted on calling it.

MINI CABRIOLET

The phenomenon of Minis with the roof missing was not a new one; Crayford produced the best known versions. However, none was officially approved until June 1991. German Rover dealer LAMM Autohaus produced a Cabriolet based on the Mini Cooper and just 75 were imported into the UK as limited edition models. Although the running gear was Cooper, the interior was Mini Mayfair, the dashboard timber and the car was finished off with a body kit.

Rover followed this limited edition a year later with an even more official Cabriolet, launched in October 1992 at the Birmingham International Motor Show. Again based on the Cooper 1.3i, it was developed by Rover Special Products and German coachbuilder Karmann, and built this time at Longbridge. The impressive strengthening work comprised an extra sill made of thick steel. This covered the standard inner sill, which meant that there were three sills in all. Tied to the extra sill was an extra-strong cross member, which ran, as it does on the standard Mini, under the front seats. The footwells on the Cabriolet were narrower than on the standard car because reinforcement plates were welded into the area where the A pillars met the sills and floor structure. The A pillars also had a steel tube running inside them. And

while the standard Mini has cubby holes underneath the rear seat, a continuous sheet of steel reinforced the rear of the floorpan. Not only that, a U-shaped sheet steel structure surrounded the rear seats, and the B posts were also substantially reinforced.

All that extra metal and the folding roof structure itself added 154lb (70kg) to the standard Cooper's 1,521lb (690kg) kerb weight. The roof was colour-coded, manually operated and folded back onto the parcel shelf. The rear windows wound down into the bodywork and disappeared completely to make a truly open car. What a shame that the Himalayan-high hood perched at the rear made passengers feel claustrophobic. It looked fairly similar on the outside to the LAMM version because it too had a prominent body kit. The alloy wheels were Revolution $12 \times 5B$ five spokes, held on with lockable wheel nuts. There was extensive chroming on the door and boot handles, spotlamps, number plate lamp cover and 'Cabriolet' script kick plates.

The specification was, as befitted the most expensive production Mini ever, luxurious. The interior was dominated by a burr walnut dashboard, comprising three main dials and an analogue clock. The timber theme extended to the door caps, door pulls and gear knob. Cut-pile carpet covered the interior, unique high back, non-tilt seats were covered in Chevron trim. The driver gripped a leather steering wheel and was restrained by colour-keyed seat belts. There were just two colour schemes: Caribbean Blue with a grey hood, or Nightfire Red with a red hood. Keeping it all safe were an alarm-coded stereo, vehicle identification numbers etched on the glass and a locking petrol cap.

Car Magazine were not impressed when they reviewed the 1992 Birmingham Motor Show and the debut of the new model, 'Absurd looking Mini Cabriolet looks like a pram without the handle, and doesn't look any less silly when someone climbs aboard, as an inspecting Sir Graham Day proved on press day.' When they got around to road testing it in their January 1994 edition the car had not got any prettier. 'First I shall state the obvious: the Mini Cabriolet looks ridiculous and at £11,995 is ludicrously expensive. Good: now that is said, I can get on with enjoying myself.' And so they did. 'I have never driven a Mini that rides as well as this one ... Even quite large furrows in the tarmac will not knock this car off line. You can achieve impressively high average speeds ... In Britain, its outrageous price makes it an interesting chapter in the Mini's long running history, but no more.'

A 1996 Cabriolet, just a few months away from being deleted. From this angle there is less chance of seeing its decidedly pram-like profile.

That chapter came to end in October 1996. Rather than modify the model to comply with the latest emissions, noise and safety regulations, production was abandoned.

ERA TURBO

Engineering Research and Application was a great name from the past, which was acquired by the Jack Knight Group. They put together a Mini that would perform a passable impression of a Cooper S. It turned out to be the fastest Mini ever built as the familiar 1,275cc engine was boosted by a Garrett T3 turbocharger. The result was 94bhp at 6,120rpm, a claimed 0–60mph time of 7.8 seconds and a top speed of 115mph (185kph). To cope with this extra power there were new front suspension arms and damper units with ventilated front discs with servo assistance. The spoked 6 × 13 alloys were shod with 165/60 13 low profile tyres. There were distinctive body modifications with a Dennis Adams styled kit, which flared the arches, sills and added a deep front spoiler. Inside, there were high backed sports seats, a new padded dashboard and a numbered plaque.

The 1989 ERA Turbo was endorsed by Rover, so you could order one through your local dealer. The first 247 models were exported to Japan, where it proved to be very popular.

An ERA Turbo pictured outside the British Embassy in Tokyo.

13 Minimalism – Buying and Tweaking

'You can make a Mini into anything: limo, rally car, U-boat, whatever you want really.'

anonymous Mini owner

In the harsh light of modern superminis, the little Mini is quite slow, crude and cramped, although it still makes a great deal of sense as a second-hand car. In pure financial terms, nothing else is cheaper to run. Parts are plentiful, insurance comparatively low and servicing is well within the DIY grasp. A well maintained Mini also has a reassuring reluctance to break down. And when it comes to selling your beloved Mini there is usually a disorderly queue of eager buyers.

Best of all, if there is something about your Mini that you do not like, change it. More than any other car a Mini can be modified to match your personality, with an almost infinite number of tweaks to make it go faster, handle better, stop quicker and look funkier. A Mini can be anything you want, the only limit being your imagination.

WHICH MINI?

There are millions to choose from, but maybe only one or two will be just right for you.

Mark I, 1959–67 There are, amazingly, plenty of survivors from the 1960s still being used as daily runabouts. Some are a bit rusty and go quite cheaply, others are tagged as 'classics' and have a price to match. Certainly the most pure Mini – just as Issigonis intended with big door bins, sliding windows and magic wand gear lever – is the Mark I. It is worth considering if you do not mind motoring at its most basic.

Mark II, 1967–69 A few refinements but essentially as the Mark I. It had the option of a larger 1-litre engine.

Clubman, 1969–82 Its blunt fronted re-style was not successful, but it came with the 1-litre and 1100 engines. The Cooper replacement 1275GT was very tepid. The Estate is the best version: it is surprisingly useful and still sought after.

Mark III, 1969–92 With it is wind-up windows, internal door hinges and reshaped grille, this is essentially the Mini that has survived into the 1990s. Millions abound, so go for the latest model you can afford. The 1,000cc engine is the better, although the 850cc survived until 1980. In 1984 all models got front disc brakes, 12in (30cm) wheels, plastic wheel arches and a re-styled interior. Of the later standard models, the City is a very basic car and the Mayfair has the minimum amount of deep pile carpeting. Post-1988 models are all better equipped and have 1bhp more power.

Roof gutters: form a crusty ring around the roof of most Minis. Easy to repair, but you should worry if rust is eating into the roof panel itself.

Limited editions The Rover special edition frenzy can get rather confusing. The important thing to remember is not to pay over the odds for a car with a few stickers and different interior trim. Of the bunch, the 1987 Park Lane was quite classy, the Racing and Flame from 1989 are Coopers without the 1,275cc engine and the Thirty is a quality package.

1.3i, 1992 onwards These were now badged as the Sprite and Mayfair, and fitted with a fuel injected catalysed 1,275cc engine, but offer a remarkably similar driving experience to the 1959 version. Do not expect too much, and do not pay too much. A 998cc 1990 Mayfair would be better value.

HOW TO BUY A MINI

The problem with many Minis is sheer neglect; they see the inside of a workshop only when something goes wrong. Minis have the ability to keep going when the engine on more expensive cars will have expired, so even quite recent ones can be run into the ground. Bonus points then for the seller with a sheaf of service bills and a string of test certificates. However, though the mechanicals are important what is the body like? Ancient assembly techniques and proliferation of body seams mean that rust is a sad fact of Mini life, and often means that it fails the statutory annual test, especially on the floorpan and rear sub-frame. Once serious rot sets in the only cure is to throw the car away. If you are a bit handy, buying two and indulging in some cannibalization is often the cheapest way to keep an old Mini alive.

Dealers like to sell Minis because there is a constant demand. However, their prices tend to reflect this. If you can, try and buy from a reliable, one-owner, private source. Such cars usually stay in the family and get looked after. With older models, always pay very careful attention to the condition.

BUYING A MINI COOPER

On the face of it, there ought to be a straightforward choice between a classic Cooper and a Rover Cooper. However, it is

Mini check points

Bodywork Look for rust, even on very recently built Minis, especially all the seams and roof channels. The front wings are especially prone; check near the headlamps and where they join the screen panel. The sills are structural items and should be checked from inside the car and underneath. While there, look at the rear sub-frame – a common test fail point. Door bottoms rust alarmingly, usually from the inside out. Look at the A panel between the door and wing: this takes the weight of the door and can corrode very badly. The offside rear window gets clogged up and rusty when parked by the pavement. Lift the carpets and look at the floor panels: moisture collects there and rust is serious. If repairs have taken place is the metal surrounding the repair plates sound? Check the boot floor, as the combination of water and battery acid can leave the battery dangling by its terminals. For some reason metallic colours seem to harbour rust more than solid finishes.

Engine The A series unit is very reliable, but when severely worn there will be serious oil leaks, noisy tappets, a rattling timing chain and smoking exhaust. Look around the engine bay for leaks, especially from the lower half of the engine; watch for damaged or missing engine steady bar rubbers and soggy engine mounts; these allow the unit to rattle around, resulting in manifold damage. The radiators can clog up, so look for signs of overheating and watch the temperature gauge on the test drive.

Drivetrain and running gear On high-mileage models the gear change will be imprecise, and the car will slip easily out of gear when accelerating. Clicking driveshafts are very common when on full lock. Listen out for clonking when accelerating, which points to worn universal joints. Crunching indicates that the synchromesh rings are worn out.

Suspension and brakes Visibly check the track rods if you can, as they can get bent when the car connects with the kerb. On a hoist, pull on the wheels to check for play and possible bearing trouble, and look for signs of wear in the rear trailing arms. Finally, take a look at the rear drum brake backing plates for leaking slave cylinders.

Floor pan: the interior of a used Mini is rarely as chaotic as this, but rust will attack the edges where the floor meets the sills. 'Flintstone' floors are quite common.

not that simple and although they are all brilliant little cars, some are more brilliant than others.

Classic Cooper Available from 1961, the 997cc is now the rarest of the plain old Coopers and if genuine, is valued accordingly. The weak spot is the engine: it is torquey but not too strong, and spares are very hard to come by. Dynamically the least exciting Cooper, this is in fact the most collectible. In 1964 the stronger and faster 998cc engine was installed. In Mark I form this is the most desirable and practical derivative. The Mark II version in 1967 with larger rear lights and windows was less individual than earlier models: with black upholstery rather than two-tone, they became even harder to distinguish from the standard Minis. As a result these versions are worth less than the Mark I, which makes them potentially the most affordable Cooper although they are by far the rarest of the breed. Provided they are intact, original and rust free, this is the best choice if you want to start classic Coopering.

Classic Cooper S The first two versions – the 1,071cc in 1963 and the 970cc in 1964 – are the two rarest Coopers, but not the most expensive or sought after. Purists might prefer them, but they are not quite as smooth or unfussed as the later 1,275cc from 1964. So they do seem to be something of a bargain, provided you can find the genuine article for sale. It is difficult to argue with the majority who opt for the 1275S, which is a very usable package indeed. Like the Cooper, in Mark II guise the appearance is more reserved, but the performance untouched. The Mark III in 1969 was even more discreet – indistinguishable from a 1,000cc shopping car and even losing the Austin and Morris branding. If you want character and not just a fast Mini then go for the Mark I or II.

Rover Cooper limited edition Those of the investment inclination would be advised to stick these models. Just over 1,000 were built and there was a good standard specification with the added bonus of 'signed' John Cooper bonnet stripes. Although more highly prized and valuable than the standard production model, there are no large profits in the short term, so it would be a shame to stick one of these in a garage and not have some fun with it.

Subframes: whereas the front subframe is lubricated by engine oil leaking from the A series engine, the rear one is vulnerable to rust and is a common MOT fail point.

Underbonnet: the bulkhead, especially around the brake and clutch fluid reservoirs, gets very rusty. Check the inner wings too. The engine is habitually oily unless recently overhauled.

Boot: like the floorpan, this collects water and rots. The battery box, thanks to spilt acid, is the first to go. Remove the battery and prod carefully.

Sills: detachable sill syndrome gets every Mini in the end. It is cheap to rectify provided the rust damage has not spread too far.

Panel/door hinges: a popular place for rust to attack Mark I Minis in particular.

Rover Cooper To some, the production models are little more than a marketing exercise, featuring a special edition model (usually a Flame or Racing) with a 1,275cc engine on board. What you are really paying for is the Cooper cachet. Nevertheless, these models are the easiest to find and provide practical everyday fun rather than the nervous pleasure of using a precious classic. The original cars without catalysts are great fun and can be cheap. The more recent 1.3i makes up for the catalytic power loss with fuel injection. If all you want to do is enjoy a Cooper rather than fuss and fettle over it, the Rover Cooper is the one to go for.

HOW TO BUY A COOPER

The considered reply is 'very carefully indeed'. The counterfeit Cooper industry is alive and flourishing and ready to trap the unwary. The best advice, especially if you want to buy a classic Cooper, is to join a club, read all the books and become a complete Cooper bore. The Mini Cooper Register's full colour, excellently produced *Buyer's Guide* is highly recommended. Everything you could possibly want to know is included.

It is impossible to give every possible identifying Cooper feature, but there are some things you should bear in mind about the seller and the car. When buying a classic Cooper the most reassuring thing that you can see is plenty of history – ideally one caring owner for the last decade or so. The documentation should back up the Cooper provenance. It is one thing to have a Cooper, Cooper S, or Limited Edition Rover Cooper specification, but quite another to find that the registration document indicates that beneath it all there is a Mini City.

Wings/headlamps: bubbles begin around the headlamp and seams where the front wing meets the front grille panel.

Possibly the hardest fake to uncover is one that has been built to match the registration document of a scrapped car. That is when you really need to put your spotter bobble hat on. The bad signs are several recent owners, restoration work of a major nature and no Heritage certificate. These certificates are issued by the British Motor Industry Heritage Trust, who keep production records

---

Counterfeit Cooper?

For novice Cooper spotters, here are some of the major Cooper clues, but these features and numbers are by no means exhaustive.

Mark I Coopers have two-tone paintwork, chrome trim around the door windows and bumpers with corner bars. The Austin grille has ten slats and the Morris has seven. In the boot there is a boot board with four support brackets riveted to the floor. Inside, there is two-tone upholstery, a three-dial instrument cluster, a 100mph speedometer, black vinyl on top of the dashboard, and a remote chrome gear lever. Chassis number prefixes are Austin C-A2S7, Morris K-A2S4. The Cooper S has a 120mph speedometer, while original S engines have removable tappet covers on rear of block with ten studs and one bolt fixing for the cylinder head.

Mark II Coopers have a seven-slatted grille and black upholstery. Bumpers have overriders but no end pieces. The Cooper S now has twin fuel tanks and a 130mph speedometer. The chassis prefix is now C-A2SB and K-A2S6. The Mark III Cooper S is as the Mini 1000 with larger rear side windows and single-colour paintwork with interior coded. The chassis prefix for Cooper, no longer Austin or Morris, is XAD–1. No Mark III had an L or later registration suffix. Rover Cooper chassis numbers SAXXNNAMBBD 011001 to 031549 distinguish it from the limited edition, which had the numbers BAD 010001 to 011050.

that detail the model and specification – very helpful, but not a guarantee of authenticity.

Finally, your nights slaving over a Cooper textbook will have you checking identifying features, chassis and engine numbers. It really depends on just how obsessive you are. Very few Coopers, especially as this is a car that begs to be driven hard, raced and rallied, will have survived completely intact over twenty or thirty years. New sub-frames, body panels and even engines are consumable items that will inevitably be replaced. Just do your very best to make sure that the seller is not telling lies, or deliberately trying to mislead you by selling a counterfeit Cooper.

MINI TUNING

No other car has been the subject of such intensive mechanical tweaking as the Mini. Daniel Richmond of Downton is credited with much of the early work as he stretched the A series engine to achieve so much more than its original designer Bill Appleby could ever have imagined.

Wing/windscreen join: rust at the junction of the wing and windscreen is common. Easy when the holes are in the wing; remove and repair. It is much more complex and expensive when the windscreen scuttle panel is crumbly.

Filler: a smoothish red pimpled finish where a seam, or panel join ought to be suggests a DIY repair with some filler.

Check points – Mini Cooper

Bodywork Rust gets its teeth into all Minis early on. The sills are good place to start. On a well cared for car it will not have spread much further, but on a neglected model check the inner wing and floor pan. The base of the door catches the disease next, and older vehicles with the bins may have drain holes blocked, which turns it into a colander. Then look at where the door attaches to the A-panel – once rotten, it will have to be replaced. The older exposed hinge doors are very susceptible. Miniologists will know that the sliding windows of the Mark I and II are fertile breeding grounds for moss, which propagates rot. The most obvious rust magnets are the gutters and seams that encircle the body. At the back, examine the valance below the bumper, as rust spreads from there into the boot and wheel arches, while the boot lid corrodes from the hinges. At the front the wings are among the first parts of a Mini to disintegrate, so look around the lights and at the top of the wings where they join the screen. Check Rover Coopers for rust and poor paintwork: there have been numerous complaints about the lack of effective quality control on early models.

Interior If you find serious rot on the outside then there will be plenty on the inside. The front footwells, under the passenger and where the wheel arches attach to the floorpan are the most likely areas. All trim on classic Coopers can be replaced, but at a price. Make sure it is as original as possible.

Engine The great (or possibly really dreadful) thing about the A series engines fitted to Minis is that they still work, even when technically worn out. The oil pressure gauges fitted to earlier cars are not always reliable, but 15psi on tickover, 40psi on the move, up to 60psi or over for a 1,275cc are the rough guides. Otherwise it is simply a case of looking for serious oil leaks, especially at the back of the block. Watch out for blue smoke from the exhaust, which suggests worn bores, and listen for the rumble of big ends that are about to expire.

Gearbox Where would we be without that distinctive whining from the Mini gearbox? But it must not be excessive. The synchromesh, especially on second, may disappear with age. Also, tired old boxes become sloppy and slip out of gear easily. That means it is time for an overhaul.

Suspension Ensure that the Mini sits level, especially the Hydrolastic sprung models (1964 to 1969). The system may need overhaul or complete replacement with the original and current dry-cone system. However, these can still sag, squeak and seize. Any odd behaviour on the test drive, indeed anything but the usual leech-like qualities of the Mini, must be investigated and might point to a previous accident.

Brakes and driveshafts A neglected car will have problems in this area, usually seized brake cylinders. The rear drum set-ups will rust in time, while the front discs can wear very thin. Listen for knocking sounds on the move, especially on full lock, which mean that the CV joints need replacing.

The number of products that can make a Mini go faster, handle better and look less than standard is almost endless, but here are just some items to tempt an enthusiastic Mini owner to investigate further. The following upgrades, packages and products show you what can be done and are available from the best known Mini specialists in the world, Mini Sport. Talk to the experts, read dedicated A series tuning books, do not cut corners and remember that at the heart of all this is a very simple power unit that can be tuned cost-effectively.

Engine The A series engine is one of the

Tuning example

A good example is the Mini Sport Injection Tuning Kit, which increases power by 35 per cent and makes a standard 1.3i Mini faster, smoother and quieter at cruising speeds. The kit comprises a specifically designed Engine Control Unit (ECU) board, which incorporates a re-programmable microchip. This new board fits directly into the existing Rover ECU casing. Then there is the modified performance cylinder head, which is fully balanced, gas flowed and polished, with larger inlet valves and an increased compression ratio. With that comes a cylinder head replacement gasket set, while a K & N air filter element increases the air flow and replaces the original paper element. Finally, a Mini Sport Superflow rear exhaust system improves gas flow and increases power, yet retains the standard catalytic converter. This fits onto the existing exhaust mountings.

---

most tuneable ever produced. The simplest way to improve performance is to replace it; the number of second-hand A series units around is astonishing. When buying a used engine, hear it running first! If you have an 850cc engine, then the easiest uprate is a 998cc, which has just 4bhp more. Do not ignore the 1,098cc unit used mainly in the Clubman, which is mated to a better gearbox. The cylinder head, carburettors and camshafts are easy swaps among the Sprite and MG 1100 family of cars for improved performance. After fiddling with the head, twin choke carburettors make a big difference, followed by a revised exhaust manifold and finally a sportier camshaft. The 1,275cc unit is quite torquey and strong, and will slot straight in from rotted-out 1275GTs and 1300GTs. These engines can more easily overheat, so the correct radiator and fan set-up must be used. However, if you do replace or uprate an engine, you must carry out essential modifications to the brakes and possibly suspension (see below). Engine tuning is an art, and a novice needs expert guidance. Buying a co-ordinated package that provides proven results is the simplest way to achieve better performance.

Gearbox The general rule is that later gearboxes are better, especially all-synchromesh ones. The 1300GT unit has long been a favourite of tuners, while Cooper gearboxes offer the closest ratios. Another way of varying performance is to take the final drive ratio and speedometer from another model with the higher or lower ratio that you require. The Mini engine has been crying out for an extra gear ever since 1959. The 1997 Mini addressed some of the high speed cruising cacophony problem with a very long fourth gear, but the ideal solution has always been an extra cog. Aftermarket five-speed boxes have been available since the 1960s, but Mini Sport came up with their own design for the 1990s. The gearbox is supplied fully assembled into a modified rod change type casing, complete with all the gears, bearings, shafts and final drive assembly, ready to bolt straight on.

Brakes Minis can always be persuaded to go faster, but in bringing them to a halt critics have always pointed out that the brakes can be a little disappointing. Uprating the brakes is not always straightforward, as the basic parts are not interchangeable without some modification. If your Mini has the old drum and drum set-up, discs would be a good idea, but the whole hub, CV joints and callipers from a later Mini will have to be used. Fitting a servo, so that less pedal pressure is required, and harder brake linings to reduce fade might be a good idea. Mini Sport have addressed the braking problem by producing their own 4 Pot calipers. Made from high grade aluminium billets, these are lightweight machined items. Each calliper is anodized for protection against corrosion and assembled with stainless steel bolts for durability. The result is extra stopping power without increased braking effort. They are direct bolt-on replacements designed for single line fitting, for use with vented discs in all wheel sizes.

Handling One thing the Mini can never be accused of is sub standard handling, but once the engine power is substantially increased the normal set-up can become a bit of a handful. Harder shock absorbers will make a difference, but the ride will become unbearable. Lowering the suspension is a cheap and cheerful route, and makes a Mini handle flatter. Mini Sport have developed their own Performance Handling Pack. It includes their own specially designed front and rear Adjusta-Ride suspension with Spax gas adjustable shock absorbers. Mini Sport's own rear wheel spacers and studs, plus five low profile Yokohama 165/60R12 A510 tyres, complete the package.

ACCESSORY MAGNET

To every accessory manufacturer, garden shed-based inventor and novelty joke emporium the Mini was a beautifully blank canvas. The minimalist interior touches and simple exterior cried out for embellishment. The Mini became a one-model accessory boom as thousands of companies solved millions of real or imagined shortfalls. Here is the tip of what was a very large gadget iceberg. Luggage space was a major preoccupation in the early 1960s, and the Mini proved interior packaging could be an art form. However, S. Reid Ltd came up with some pyramid-shaped suitcases that fitted into the tiny boot. Roof racks were plonked on top to increase

stowage space in a high rise manner. Worst of all, a glass fibre boot extension from Sackville may have incorporated the original boot lid, but it still looked like a nasty carbuncle on the bottom of a good friend.

Anticipating the four-wheel-drive boom, companies like Desmo came up with a spare wheel carrier, which mounted it on the lid and freed up some space in the wheel well. Interestingly, others came up with genuine innovations that would be copied by BMC, like an internal bonnet release. Speedwell came up with a long range fuel tank that added 5 gallons (22 litres) to the capacity and seat extensions gave at least 2in (51mm) more leg-room for the front seat occupants. Remote gear changes from SPQR and Sackville were a big improvement over the magic wand that was a standard fit on the non-Coopers. Wind-up windows were on offer long before BMC got around to fitting them. Owners who kept the door bin could fit armrests and choose between dozens of alternative door handles, which replaced the length of liquorice used on Mark I and II Minis. (Some updates were not quite so useful, including rear wheel arch spats, sun visors, chrome peaks for the headlamps and a wood-grained plastic dashboard.)

Once the real professionals went to town, like Harold Radford in the 1960s and Wood & Pickett in the 1970s, the Mini became lost under the weight of gadgets and frills. Yet a Mini was never better served than when owners stamped their own personality on the car. Wider wheels, lairy paintwork, furry seats – whatever they did was fine.

Performance modifications remain a preoccupation in the 1990s. Those who can afford a new Mini, though, like the factory touches, which only encourages Rover to come up with even more special editions. At least it is reassuring to know that there is no such thing as a standard Mini. It is whatever you want it to be.

14 Minllennium – Car of the Century

*'The Mini is the only lovable small car.
The others are just like bars of soap.'*

Bernd Pischetsrieder (BMW Chairman, 1996)

The Mini is simply the perfect small car. Whether you want to do the shopping, get into motorsport, or express your own outgoing personality with a paint job and snazzy seat covers, then you can do no better than buy a Mini. It is a cheap and infinitely cheerful way to go motoring, but it so much more than just a car. Here are a few suggestions as to why the Mini is still with us after all these years.

THE MINI AS DESIGN ICON

Any designer who has to justify their new small car has one major hurdle – it will inevitably be compared unfavourably with the Mini. Park any contemporary supermini next to the original and they look overweight, over-complicated and completely over the top. As the first chapter of this book makes clear, the Mini was not styled or designed in the conventional sense: the bodywork did nothing more than clothe the mechanics to produce a shape. You can see the joins, but they define the shape so that it is not an amorphous or cute town car, but a vehicle with a purpose and, most important, an edge. Arch anti-stylist Issigonis had the last laugh as the 1959 bodywork

has yet to reach its sell-by date. Every design cliché can be thrown at the Mini, yet the Mini is an original. It is unique.

Other manufacturers liked the idea, looked at the sales and finally the bottom line before running scared. Ford have waited until the 1990s to launch the Ka, confident that it can make a profit and that there is a market niche for a car with no discernible purpose apart from being small, distinctive and fashionable. The Ka is intended to be a 1990s Mini. It is resoundingly better than the Mini in many areas. But icons usually happen by accident, rather than by design.

CLASSLESS MINI

It has been said 'you are what you drive', this also means that what you drive says a lot about you. Roll up in a Ford and you must be a sales rep, a Volvo Estate and you must be an antique dealer. In a Mini you could be anyone at all. The only other vehicle to pull off this trick is the Land Rover, equally at home on the farm with fertilizer in the back or stuffed with champers and hampers at a Polo meet. It is the same for the Mini, anyone can and does get away with driving it. Issigonis was proved completely wrong when he

(Above) *Mini: a natural novelty magnet.*

(Right) *The Ford Ka. A thoroughly modern Mini?*

envisaged the toiling classes flocking to put a Mini-Minor outside their homes. In fact the whole novelty of the package intrigued the middle and upper classes as well as those clever media types and personalities. Peter Sellers, Spike Milligan, George Harrison and Princess Grace of Monaco all chose to put a Mini outside their homes. Small did not have to mean cheap, the Mini was fashion. It was beautiful. It was classless.

HEROIC MINI

We love the underdog in Britain. Someone up against the odds, the Dunkirk spirit and stiff upper lip. The underdog doesn't even have to win, or even come second, they just have to put up a darned good show. On the race track and in rallying the image of this terrier-like Cooper snapping at the heels of the larger and more powerful machinery was inspiring. But the Mini did not just put up a darned good show, it won the whole thing. Regularly. And convincingly. When the Mini was disqualified on a 'technicality' after the Mini Monte 1–2–3 in 1966 it only made the little car more famous. It was a proud time, and we knew who had really won the Monte. Just to make the point the Mini won again in 1967.

You don't need a full-face helmet, roll cage and competition harness to get a buzz from owning, or driving a Mini. You only need to complete a journey, especially a long one to be praised and appreciated. The fact that something so small and apparently vulnerable can cope, let alone thrive, in a modern motoring environment is a remarkable achievement. We need heroes. We need Minis.

MINI AS A BEST PAL

Auto Anthropomorphism. The sad case of people attributing human qualities to their cars. But it happens, a Mini is much more than an inanimate object. Like the VW Beetle and Morris Minor, the Mini has an attractively rounded shape at the front end that suggests a face but it is more capable than either. Not only can you not help smiling when you see a Mini, you cannot help smiling when you drive one.

Is it possible to be too sentimental about Minis? Not according to British Leyland who came up with the 'Minis have feelings too' slogan and the kissing Minis TV campaign. It worked. Instead of addressing the technological and refinement shortfalls of the Mini they reminded us the car was still there and still lovable. Buying a Mini is always going to be an emotional rather than a logical desision. In effect the Mini is the best friend you will ever have.

MINI AS A MEDIA STAR

Lights, Camera, Action. The Mini is a natural when it comes to being photographed, or

This cheesy publicity shot only works because the Mini is lovable and cannot be embarrassed.

A novel way of demonstrating the huge Mini range in an unidentified early 1960s BMC showroom.

filmed. It is the quintessential British car, eccentric, small and endearing and perfect for film directors who want a quick reference to Britishness. Along with the red double-decker, black taxi and Beefeaters, nothing sums a nation up more than a quirky small car driving on the 'wrong' side of the road. In *Four Weddings and a Funeral*, the first wedding dash to Devon happens courtesy of an MOT borderline Mini. However, few cars can lay claim to a starring role in a major motion picture. Roll forward the three Mini Coopers which dominated *The Italian Job*.

Any film that can bring together the talents of Hollywood star Micheal Caine, music hall stalwart Fred Emney, the bawdy humour of Benny Hill and the stiff upper lip of Renaissance man Sir Noel Coward, had to be brilliant. The film itself was an amusing insight into the Brits abroad with plenty of Union

Jacks, beer and football. The bad guys were the Mafia and the Minis were the perfect cars for the bullion job. No other UK car would fit the bill. It had to be a Mini, for a start the bullion was destined for Fiat and there was no better way to show up the Polizi Alfas than with a pack of screaming red, white and blue Cooper Ss. The Italian Job = Mini. It was the best 90-minute advert the Mini ever had, it is still shown twice a year, and you still end up watching it.

Minis might disappear from the road, but they will never go away.

LATEST AND LAST?

If anyone was concerned that the Mini had fallen into the wrong hands when BMW took on Rover, they need not have worried. Bernd

Pischetsrieder, the BMW Chairman did not just love the Mini but believed it had a future. Interviewed for the February 1996 issue of *Car Magazine* by Gavin Green, Pischetsrieder had very definite views on its image and future: 'The Mini has a brand image which is totally apart from Rover. I think it's crazy to call the car the Rover Mini, or even hint that's what it's called. The car has been called an Austin Mini, a Morris Mini, a Wolseley Mini, a Riley Mini and God knows what else. With all due respect, that's bullshit. A Mini is a Mini. And because it's a brand name, it could be a family of cars. Alec's idea was to minimize resources. The new car must also be limited to the essentials. It'll be recognizably a Mini, even though it will be all new. The Mini is the only lovable small car. The others are just like bars of soap.'

The next generation of Minis was already underway, but it was enjoying several false starts. Project R59, involving both BMW and Rover engineers, was to have resulted in a British styled but German engineered Mini relying on existing small car set-ups. The project was renamed E50 when Munich assumed control as the car went over budget and beyond its sign off deadline so that the launch date went beyond 1998 and on to 2000.

MINI 1997

Meanwhile, Rover made sure that the existing Mini was dramatically re-engineered for the first time since 1959. Its development had effectively stood still since 1969 (with the introduction of wind-up windows, concealed door hinges and Clubman fronts being the last radical changes). So, 1 October 1996 was the launch date and the Paris Motor Show was the revised Mini's debut.

The changes signified Rover's appreciation that the Mini was a brand in its own right (there were new 'Mini' badges but not

The 1997 models come in just two flavours. The Mini is pictured with an optional canvas sunroof and the Cooper with optional sports pack.

a Rover logo in sight) and that buyers enjoyed individualizing their cars with a large range of options. The Mini had arrived as a premium price niche product and Rover were prepared to admit it. According to their press release: 'Throughout the 1990s, Mini has been moving steadily upmarket. In the key export markets of Europe and Japan, Mini has long been perceived as a desirable status symbol, bought for its heritage and unique, ageless style. The 1997 programme moves the UK versions of the car in this same direction, as there are no longer any "entry-level" models such as the previous Sprite, or low price Special Editions.'

It went on: 'Typical Mini buyers are now less likely to be families seeking a second, or third car, but increasingly tend to be single,

Sports pack equipped Cooper on the move, but slower because of all those extra bits.

(Below) A 1997 Mini Cooper. 'Every Boy's Dream' is the caption. Are the boys still dreaming, or are they looking forward to a better Mini in the 21st Century?

well-educated professional and managerial people desiring a fashion statement. The 1997 Mini sees an important step-change in the development and projection of the Mini brand by reverting to a classically simple and straightforward range that emphasizes the strength of the brand, taking it firmly upmarket.'

MINI RE-ENGINEERED

Leaving aside the marketing copy and the cosmetic frills we will come to later, the most significant changes were in the most important area of all, under the bonnet. The 1,275cc Cooper engine was made standard for the 1997 models, with multi-point fuel injection. This was controlled by the MEMS 2J engine management system (as developed for the 2.5-litre KV6 and MGF 1.8i VVC engines) to give a fully programmed sequential injection. Each injector was pulsed at the optimum time to fuel independently the cylinders that it served. This provided precise control of the fuel input and distribution to achieve very low emissions without any loss in performance.

There was also a direct electronic ignition system using quad dry-coil twin-spark technology, which triggered each spark twice, once on the compression stroke and once on the exhaust. This meant that the high tension voltage did not have to be switched between cylinders. The cylinder block itself was modified to delete the distributor housing and it also involved a redesign of the oil galleries and relocation of the oil filter. This allowed the radiator to be moved from its traditional side mounting to a more conventional position in front of the engine as part of the pass-by noise reduction programme (*see* below). Also new under the bonnet was the replacement of the 45amp alternator with a 65amp version and the use of a poly vee belt alternator and water pump drive for greater durability and reliability.

All these changes resulted in the cleanest A series unit ever, matching the power and torque figures of the previous Cooper unit, but at lower engine speeds. For lower internal noise levels, a 2.76:1 final drive ratio raised the overall gearing by 16 per cent compared to the previous Cooper. The higher kerb weight (it was up by 3.5 per cent)

meant that the performance suffered, but not by much. The old Cooper had a maximum speed of 92mph (148kph), the new 90mph (145kph), and 0–60mph took 11.5 seconds in the old days and 12.2 seconds for the 1997 model. Fourth gear was now claimed to be the equivalent to most fifth gears as it cut engine speed at 70mph (113kph) from 3,888rpm to 3,333rpm. As a result of all these changes, the automatic transmission, which had always been a costly item to produce, was dropped.

SAFE AND SECURE

Apart from the mechanical changes, probably the most welcome changes were those relating to safety and security. The Mini is often criticized for being easy to steal (as well as being small and vulnerable, although many owners will testify to the car's strength and manoeuvrability). Rover addressed these shortfalls for 1997 specification Minis. So secondary safety equipment involved some complex engineering. A driver's airbag was fitted as standard and seat belt pre-tensioners (actuated by pyrotechnic devices in the inertia reel units) and side door intrusion beams were part of the core specification on both models. The airbag required a total redesign of the steering column, enabling the fitment of column control stalks to bring the lighting switches within fingertip control of the driver at long last.

On the security side there was a full perimetric alarm system, plus an engine immobilizer, operated by a remote control. Even if the owner forgets or delays the setting of the system, the engine immobilser will be automatically activated after a few seconds. A fascia warning light flashed once the system was activated as a visible deterrent. The new steering column also incorporated a new lock.

The view under a 1997 Mini bonnet with multi-point fuel injection, radiator sited in front of the engine, repositioned oil filter and bigger alternator.

(Below)
Inside a 1997 Mini, which has never been so luxurious (or safe, for that matter). Cosmetically there is stone beige leather, wood accessory pack and wood gear knob. Note the chunkier air bagged steering wheel, plus column stalks, in the familiar bus driving position.

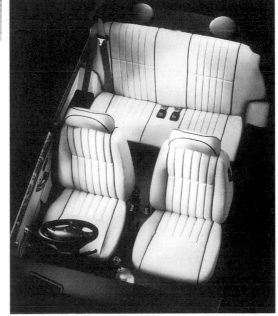

REFINED MINI

The Mini also became quieter – under a new EU Directive, all cars registered after October 1996 must not exceed a noise level of 74dB(A), down from 77dB(A). That might not sound much, but according to Rover it represented a halving of the prevailing noise levels. To achieve this the 1997 Mini's higher gearing, front mounted radiator with electric cooling fan and rear exhaust silencer box were all part of the package.

Inside, there were numerous sound-deadening measures including damping pads in the roof, plus the new foam-backed fabric headlining, which helped to tune out the 'boom' effect at higher engine speeds. Extra sound path sealing around the top of the bulkhead and the A-post areas kept engine noise out and new sound insulation around the fuel tank and boot area eliminated any possibility of whine from the high-pressure fuel pump. The rear seat bulkhead was now solid, as the blanked off aperture was deleted from the pressing. Improved acoustic insulation from road noise resulted from a new moulded one-piece floor carpet.

MAXI – ACCESSORIES

Rover did not miss a trick when it came to specification for 1997 Minis – there were 37 different 'personalizing' items. Rover viewed the situation like this: 'For example,

retro enthusiasts might choose the prefect finishing touch of a 1960s-style grille to go with a "Classic" paint and trim combination. "Thoroughly modern" Mini buyers may choose high tech treatment, with "chrome" wheel arches complementing the special alloy wheel sets. The natural extroverts may opt for a striking decal treatment, such as the chequered roof panel. The potential is bounded only by imagination and budget, and, of course, the personalization process can continue right through the customer's ownership of the car.'

1997 MINI REVIEWED

Car Magazine were not over-impressed by the Mini revisions when they reviewed it in their Newcomers section, under the title

---

1997 Mini packs

The Sports Pack comprises 13in 6J 'Minilite Style' alloy wheels with 175/50 R13 tyres, faired-in and body-coloured wheel arch spats to cover the wide tyres, Koni shock absorbers, four front auxiliary lamps, large bore chrome tailpipe finisher and extra fascia gauges for oil temperature and battery condition. Unfortunately the extra aerodynamic drag of the wide tyres reduce the top speed to 84mph (135kph): the Cd is down from the standard car's 0.49 to 0.54 and 0–60mph time has slipped from 12.2 to 12.8 seconds.

Chrome Pack 1 has a retro-style chrome grille, front bumper overriders and corner nudge bars. Chrome Pack 2 has chrome wiper arms, door mirrors and tail pipe finisher. The Interior Pack (colour keyed red, blue, or green) offers a leather header rail, parcel shelf finisher, steering wheel, hand brake grip and gear knob. The Alloy Pack produces alloy door pulls, door releases and window winders.

The Decals Pack gives buyers a Union Jack roof, Chequered roof, 'Zipper' side stripe or chequered bonnet stripes. Wood Pack: cappings, door pulls, door releases, window winders. Interior: engine turned fascia panel, 'Cooper' black leather trim, 'Luxury' beige leather trim. Special option 'Classic' leather trim in retro 1960s Mini interior trim colours of Porcelain Green, Horizon Blue, Cumulus Grey, Tartan Red. Exterior: Special Option Classic Paint, Almond Green, Surf Blue, Whitehall Beige, Yukon Grey.

Engine Dressing: polished rocker cover, sump guard. Wheels: 12in sports style in Silver, charcoal or White; 12in Premium; 12in Revolution 5-spoke; 13in Revolution 5-spoke; 13in Sports. Sunroofs: electric glass, electric full length canvas. Standard paint colours: solid – Flame Red, White Diamond, Electric Blue; metallic – Charcoal, Platinum Silver, Kingfisher Blue, British Racing Green; pearlescent – Nightfire Red, Tahiti Blue, Amaranth (purple), Volcano (orange).

This is what the Mini had become in the late 1990s – a fashionable magnet for options. This Cooper has a chequered roof decal, bonnet stripes, exterior bright packs, white alloys, driving lamps and chrome wheel arch spats.

'Going quietly to the grave.' After recounting all the important mechanical updates, Paul Horrell summed up the major objection: 'All this engineering cost, spread over a comparatively tiny number of cars, means a price hike. Rover reckons Mini buyers are not interested in cost anyway, so it has elected to go for a boutique strategy: big prices, big range of optional trimmings and accessories, so you can't now buy a Mini for under nine grand. Gulp.' After criticizing the lengthy final drive and the sports pack, which made the Cooper slower, the summary was to be expected: 'In the year of the Ka, don't try and justify it as a sensible buy. It just isn't.'

Autocar were more positive. Writer Colin Goodwin zeroed in on the appeal of the car 'You do not buy a Mini these days because it is a small car, you buy it because it is a Mini.' The myriad options were not seen as a handicap, there was much appreciation

for the soundproofing and the fact that the fun aspect of driving a Mini had not been lost. 'Rover has provided us with the safest, most liveable-with Mini to date. It's just up to you how you finish the job.'

MINI – THE FUTURE

It is impossible and just a little futile to speculate on the next generation of Mini in the year 2000 or so. Although Bernd Pischetsrieder has given us a few clues, why not leave the last few words to Issigonis, from his report in 1973 to BL Chairman Lord Stokes, outlining the requirements for a new model: 'A new Mini replacement must set new concepts of car design as the original Mini fourteen years ago. To replace the Mini with a new one that is neither lighter nor offering more internal accommodation seems pointless.'

Stop Press: ACV 30 Anniversary Concept

Three yars after BMW's buyout of the Rover Group, the companies, publicity revealed their first joint project on January 18th 1997 in the shape of the ACV 30.

The offical line is that the AVC30 Anniverary Concept was built to commemorate the 30th anniversay of the hat-trick of Mini wins in the Monte Carlo rallies of 1964, '65 and '67, hence the classic red and white livery of the famous BMC Competitions department rally cars. Actually this concept was revealed to help Rover and BMW design and marketing departments decide how the retro-styling of the next generation Mini could look. Most important though, was judging the public's reaction, would they fall in love, or be horrified?

According to Rover sources the basic mechanical and packaging of the new Mini had been decided, but the interior and exterior design was still subject to a raging debate. Chris Bangle, BMW design chief, described the distinctly Cooperesque front end to *Car* magazine as a 'mouth spitting out four breadsticks.' What a pleasant image that conjures up. There were no offical dimensions released with the ACV30, but it is roughly the size of a Peugeot 106 which puts it at just over a foot longer than the existing Mini.

This prototype was based on the running gear of the MGF sports car which mated the front and rear subframes plus the 1.8 litre, 115bhp double overhead camshaft, 16-valve K series engine. It is mounted amidships and drives the rear wheels. The AVC was built in just four months with aluminium body panels formed in Germany by a top secret new process.

Press reaction to the AVC was universally enthusiastic. *Performance Car* magazine summed it up for everyone when they commented, 'As a publicity stunt the ACV is perfect, but we can't help thinking it's a crying shame that there's no hope of such a promising junior sports car hitting the streets.'

Stop Press II: Mini Spiritual and Spiritual Too

Dateline: 4th March 1997. Venue: Geneva International Motor Show. The Rover Group unveiled a revolutionary Mini design concept that gave the best indication yet as to how the next Mini will look. Rover believe that the concept follows the same radical thought processes used by Sir Alec Issigonis with the three-door Spiritual platform leading to a potential family of Mini cars. The Spiritual Too is just one example: a larger, one-box, five-door family saloon. The Spiritual mimics the dimensions of the original Mini being just 3.1m long (around 10ft) which not only seats four adults in comfort, but also meets prevailing and foreseeable crash regulations and emission requirements.

The greatest break with Mini tradition is the Spiritual's powerplant which is a flat, three cylinder engine mounted under the rear seats and driving the rear wheels. This will develop around 45kW, expected to reach 100km (62mph) in 13 seconds and fuel consumption of 3.0 litres to every 100km (104mpg!). The fuel tank is located under the front seats, with the spare wheel, battery and radiator in the front compartment. Like the old Metro/Rover 100, suspension is provided by the Hydragas system and the whole Spiritual package weighs just 700kg (1,575 lb).

Spiritual Too is the design study for a larger five door body utilizing the same layout and mechanical configuration as Spiritual in a 3.5m (11ft 4in), 900kg (2,025lb) package. However, the powerplant would be a flat four cylinder unit.

Rover are keen to stress that this is not the new Mini. We shall see ...

15 Minimalists

Here is a far from comprehensive listing of clubs, specialists and books that make Mini ownership and enjoyment even easier.

SPECIALISTS

The Mini Shop (parts)
385 Hertford Road, Enfield, Middlesex
EN3 5PP
Telephone 0181 805 8085

Avonbar Racing (performance parts)
219 New Haw Road, Addlestone,
Weybridge, Surrey KT15 2DP
Telephone 01932 842024

Moss (parts)
22–28 Manor Road, Richmond, Surrey
TW9 1YB
Telephone 0500 479299

MED Engineering Services (parts,
tuning)
Unit 6, 238 Tithe Street, Leicester
Telephone 0116 2461 641

Mini Spares Centre (parts)
Telephone: London 0181 368 6292,
Harrogate 01423 881800,
Midlands 0121 544 0011

Mini Sport Ltd (tuning and parts)
Thompson Street, Padiham, Lancashire
BB12 7AP
Telephone 01282 778731

Newton Commercial (interior trim)
Eastlands Industrial Estate, Leiston,
Suffolk IP16 4LL
Telephone 01728 832880

John Cooper Garages Ltd
Ferring Street, Ferring, Worthing, West
Sussex BN12 5JP
Telephone 01903 504455

Bank Garage (sales, service, parts,
restoration)
Sixteen Foot Bank, Chritchurch,
Cambridgeshire PE14 9LN
Telephone 01354 638667

BOOKS

The Complete Mini – Rees.
The Illustrated History of Works Minis in International Rallies and Races – Browning.
How to Modify Your Mini – Vizard.
Theory and Practice of Cylinder Head Modification – Vizard.
Tuning BL's A Series Engine – Vizard.
Mini: 35 Years 1959–1994 – Golding.
Mini: Restoration, Preparation, Maintenance – Tyler.
Mini Owner's Survival Manual – Tyler.
The Big Mini Book – Hubner.
Mini Cooper: The Real Thing! – Tipler.
Mini Purchase and Restoration Guide – Porter.
Mini Service Guide and Owner's Manual – Porter.
Original Mini Cooper and Cooper S – Parnell.
Mighty Minis – Harvey
The Sporting Minis – Bridgen

MAGAZINES

Mini World
Link House, Dingwall Avenue, Croydon CR9 2TA
Telephone 0181 686 2599

Mini Magazine
A&S Publishing, Messenger House, 35 St Michael's Square, Gloucester GL1 1HX
Telephone 01452 307181

CLUBS

These are just a handful of the hundreds of national (and international) organizations set up to celebrate the Mini. Consult the latest issue of *Mini World* for an up to date listing:

Crayford Convertible Club
58 Geriant Road, Downham, Bromley, Kent BR1 5DX

Mini Cooper Club
59 Giraud Street, Poplar, London E14 6EE

Mini Cooper Register
60 Broad Lane, Hampton, Middlesex TW12 3BG

Mini Drivers Club
2 Eastcroft Road, Wallasey, Wirral, Merseyside

Mini Moke Club
Highgate, Leys Lane, Meriden, Warwickshire CV7 7LQ

Mini Owners Club
15 Birchwood Road, Lichfield, Staffordshire WS14 9UN

Mini Se7en Racing Club
245 Clay Lane, South Yardley, Birmingham B26 1ES

Index